contents

To my husband,

Donald Breitenberg,

for indulging

my culinary curiosity

introduction

The last decade of every century has traditionally been a time of nostalgic reflection. Perhaps this explains the returning popularity of hearty home-style cooking, often referred to as "bistro fare." There is a new value being placed on the unpretentious, soul-satisfying dishes that our grandmothers and great-grandmothers cooked for us. There is a growing demand for the enticing aromas of savory soups and stews bubbling on the top of the stove and deep-dish pies and cobblers fresh from the oven.

This concept is truly global in scope. Whether you are planning French, Italian, Greek, Scandinavian, Mexican, Asian, or regional American menus, you will usually find that the less complicated the preparation, the more tasty and satisfying it is.

Back-to-basics cooking makes use of fresh seasonal fruits and vegetables as well as dried beans and peas, grains of all types, less expensive cuts of meat, and poultry and leftovers of every description. This array of primarily low-cost ingredients makes this robust style of cooking extremely economical. These ingredients also make it ideal for even the most health-conscious cooks by simply keeping the high-fat and high-cholesterol ingredients in the proper proportion in the recipes.

In *Light and Hearty* I have not attempted to create fat-free, spa-type recipes, but rather to revise some of my own favorite bistro-style dishes from around the world using the same techniques for lowering the fat, cholesterol, and sodium that I use in revising recipes for my column, "Cook it Light." (The column is an interactive one. Readers write asking for advice, often sending a favorite family recipe that needs lightening-up. Their letters and original recipes are printed along with my answers and revised recipes every week.)

When revising recipes I always start in the same manner. I first make the original version so that I have a benchmark to test against. It is important that a revised recipe never lose the integrity of the original dish in taste, texture, or appearance. When it does, I am back to square one and have to start all over again using a different approach. Sometimes I'm lucky and the first version is right on the mark. Other times it has taken me as many as ten tries before I'm satisfied with the results. Also, there are recipes that simply cannot be revised to be lighter without sacrificing too much in taste or texture (butter cookies are a good example). In these cases I recommend making them less frequently and eating fewer of them when you do!

There are a number of "tricks" I use to lower the amount of fat in a recipe. First and foremost, you can cook in nonstick cookware or use a nonstick vegetable spray on your pans and baking dishes to prevent sticking rather than using butter, margarine, or oil. You can also substitute water, defatted stock, juice, or wine in place of oil to prevent sticking or scorching when sautéeing.

For instance, when a recipe calls for cooking onions, garlic, or shallots in butter or oil, omit the fat and cook them over low heat, covered, in a heavy saucepan or skillet until they are soft and translucent, about 10–15 minutes. Stir occasionally and add a little water, stock, juice, or wine to prevent scorching if necessary. (Extremely lightweight pans do not work for this technique.) This is called "sweating" the vegetables since they release their own moisture as they cook—sort of like "stewing in your own juices"! You will have saved a whopping 120 calories per tablespoon of fat called for, or about 14 grams of fat.

If you are making a spaghetti sauce and you want the flavor of the olive oil, you can achieve a better taste with less fat by using this sweating technique and then adding a very small amount of a wonderful, aromatic extra-virgin olive oil when you are making the final seasoning adjustments just before serving the sauce.

When making salad dressings you can replace at least half of the oil called for with water, stock, or juice and still have a very satisfying and tasty dressing.

To reduce the amount of saturated fat use liquid vegetable oils, such as olive and canola oil, and pure corn oil or safflower margarine in a tub rather than a stick. Do no use coconut oil, palm kernel oil, or bar chocolate. Many nondairy creamers contain coconut or palm kernel oil so always read the labels. For coconut flavor use coconut extract and for chocolate use powdered cocoa.

To further reduce your intake of saturated fat, buy the leanest cuts of meat available and trim off all visible fat. Always remove the skin and visible fat from poultry, and refrigerate stocks and pan drippings until the fat has congealed on the top and can be easily removed.

Buy the lowest fat dairy products available that are a viable substitute for the original ingredient called for. For example, many nonfat cheeses do not melt properly, but reduced-fat cheeses work beautifully, as do light sour cream and low-fat ricotta and cottage cheese. Canned evaporated skimmed milk is an excellent substitute for cream in many sauces.

The best way to reduce the amount of cholesterol in your diet is to eat more complex carbohydrates—such as fruits, vegetables, legumes, and grains—and less animal protein. Cholesterol is found only in foods of animal origin. There is no cholesterol in any food of plant origin. Foods particularly high in cholesterol are egg yolks and organ meats, such as liver, heart, kidneys, brains, and sweetbreads.

Tofu works surprisingly well as a substitute for mayonnaise in sauces, especially when you want more body than a nonfat or cholesterol-free mayonnaise would provide. Tofu is soybean curd. It was once used only in Asian cooking, but it is now available in all supermarkets. It is a true chameleon in the food world because it has virtually no taste of its own. It takes on the flavor of anything it is marinated in or mixed with. A good example of using tofu to replace fat is my Aïoli recipe on page 81.

Also, in recipes calling for whole eggs, you can almost always use only the whites, or at least eliminate half of the egg yolks. Substitute two egg whites for each whole egg called for in the recipe. You can substitute a better, unsaturated fat for the bad, saturated fat found in egg yolks by using a teaspoon of vegetable oil for each egg yolk eliminated. This is especially true in recipes such as cakes and cookies that call for whole eggs to provide moisture and texture. In many baked goods, you can substitute unsweetened apple sauce for at least half of the fat called for in the recipe. The cellulose in apples traps the moisture, giving much the same texture achieved by fat.

The best way to reduce the amount of sodium in your diet is to cook with more herbs and spices. We taste only four things: sweet, sour, salt, and bitter. Everything else we often call "taste" is really smell. Therefore, if you increase the aroma, you have more flavor without using as much salt. Always crush dried herbs in a mortar with a pestle before adding them to any recipe, whether hot or cold. Grind them until you can literally smell them all over the kitchen. Everything you make will be infinitely tastier and everyone will think you are a fabulous cook.

If you are on a sodium-restricted diet, avoid foods particularly high in sodium. These include most cheeses, soy sauce and many other commercial sauces and condiments, most snack foods, canned soups, and all stock bases, including bouillon cubes.

Remember, your only limitation in cooking is your own imagination. The more you learn about the many and varied cuisines of the world, the more fun you can have mixing and matching them. Staying on the cutting edge of food fashion is extremely important in my work. For this reason, I regularly travel all over the world and attend cooking schools to learn more about the techniques and ingredients used by different ethnic and cultural groups. I also serve as a consultant on light cuisine for many international hotels and spas, which affords me the opportunity to work with their talented chefs. As well as teaching, I am continuously learning from them.

Currently the most popular trend among many of the younger chefs is what some food writers are calling "fusion food" or "multicultural cuisine." They combine the ingredients of one type of ethnic food with the flavor range of another. Good examples of this cross-cultural mix are the Spicy Carrot Risotto (page 46) and the Pacific Rim Pizza Quiche (page 59).

When using these recipes, don't be limited by what should be an appetizer or an entree. Double a vegetable side dish for an entree or divide a pasta recipe by half or even a third to make a first course. The same principles work beautifully for most of the fish, poultry, and meat dishes as well. Let your own taste and menu planning preferences dictate your decisions and use the recipes in this book as a guide.

I have used all of the ingredients and techniques I have learned along the way to revise my own favorite home-style recipes for this book. They are lighter, more healthful, and smarter choices for your daily meals—without losing any of their soul-satisfying taste or heartiness!

Tom Nuea Savoey, page 6.

Velouté d'Escargot
(Cream of Snail Soup)

Cold Caviar Soup in Artichoke Bowls

Artichoke "Bowls"

Garden Patch Soup

Tom Nuea Savoey
(Thai Beef Soup with Daikon Radish)

Black Bean Soup

Split Pea Soup

Pasta e Fagioli
(Pasta and Bean Soup)

Avgolemono
(Greek Lemon Soup)

Tricolor Gazpacho

Chilled English Stilton-Pear Soup

Catalina Clam Chowder

Velouté d'Escargot

(Cream of Snail Soup)

2 tablespoons corn oil margarine

½ cup chopped shallots (2 ounces)

2 stalks celery, without leaves, finely chopped (1 cup)

¾ cup loosely packed chopped fresh parsley

2 tablespoons minced garlic (6 cloves)

½ cup unbleached all-purpose flour

⅔ cup dry white wine

2 cups defatted chicken stock

2 cups 2% low-fat milk

1 teaspoon salt (omit if using salted stock)

¼ teaspoon freshly ground white pepper

1½ teaspoons dried tarragon, crushed with a mortar and pestle

Dash of nutmeg

2 4½-ounce cans snails, rinsed, drained, and chopped (1¼ cups)

1 teaspoon fresh lemon juice

8 snail shells, for garnish (optional)

8 sprigs fresh tarragon, for garnish (optional)

Try this delightfully different presentation of escargot. Many people a bit put off by digging snails out of shells—even ceramic shells—will enjoy this rich-tasting soup. It makes a marvelous first course for a light luncheon menu when served with a cold salad entree.

1. Melt the margarine in a heavy saucepan over low heat. Add the shallots, celery, parsley, and garlic and cook, covered, until soft, stirring occasionally. Add the flour and mix well. Continue to cook for 2 minutes, stirring constantly to prevent scorching.

2. Increase the heat to medium and add the wine. Mix well and cook until nearly all the wine has evaporated. Slowly add the stock and milk, stirring frequently until the mixture comes to a boil. Reduce the heat to low and simmer, stirring constantly, until thickened. Add the salt, pepper, tarragon, and nutmeg and mix well.

3. Remove from the heat and add the snails and lemon juice. Mix well and serve immediately. If reheating the soup, heat to serving temperature but do not boil or the snails will be tough.

4. To serve, fill each of eight bowls with ¾ cup soup and garnish with a snail shell and a sprig of fresh tarragon, if desired.

Makes 6 cups; eight ¾-cup servings

Each serving contains approximately:

Calories: 135   **Cholesterol: 19 mg**

Fat: 5 g   **Sodium: 417 mg**

Cold Caviar Soup in Artichoke Bowls

1 envelope (1 tablespoon)
  unflavored gelatin

2 tablespoons cold water

1/4 cup boiling water

1/2 cup nonfat (skim) milk

1 cup defatted beef stock

1/2 cup light sour cream

1 tablespoon fresh lemon juice

4 ounces salmon caviar

1/2 cup minced onion

2 hard-boiled eggs, whites
  only, shredded

4 Artichoke "Bowls" (page 4)

Chives, for garnish (optional)

This soup is a great way to make a little bit of caviar go a long way. When serving soup in artichoke bowls always explain to your guests that most of the soup should be eaten before eating the sides of the bowl!

1. Soften the gelatin in the cold water. Add the boiling water and stir until the gelatin is completely dissolved. Add the milk and stock and mix well. Place the gelatin mixture in a covered container in the refrigerator until it has jelled.

2. Combine the gelatin mixture, sour cream, and lemon juice in a blender and blend until thoroughly mixed. Pour the mixture into a large bowl and add the caviar, onion, and shredded egg whites, mixing thoroughly with a wire whisk. Chill well before serving in the Artichoke "Bowls." Garnish with chives, if desired.

Makes 4 servings

Each serving contains approximately:

Calories: 130   **Cholesterol: 12 mg**

Fat: 4 g   **Sodium: 173 mg**

Artichoke "Bowls"

4 large artichokes
2 garlic cloves, halved
1 slice lemon

1. Thoroughly wash the artichokes; pull off and discard the toughest outer leaves. Cut off the thorny tips of the remaining outer leaves, then cut off the stem so the artichokes are flat on the bottom. Invert the artichokes and press down firmly to open them up as much as possible.

2. In a saucepan large enough to hold the artichokes, pour water to a depth of 2 inches. Add the garlic and lemon, then bring to a boil. Place the artichokes in the boiling water flat side down, cover the pan tightly, and cook over medium heat until the stem end can be easily pierced with a fork, about 40 minutes. Remove the artichokes from the water and place upside down to drain until cool enough to handle.

3. Remove the center leaves, then very carefully spread the artichokes open to expose the hearts. Remove the small heart leaves and, with a spoon, scrape out the furry chokes to make clean, edible artichoke "bowls." Fill as desired.

Makes 4 "bowls"

Each "bowl" contains approximately:

Calories: 53	**Cholesterol: None**
Fat: Negligible	**Sodium: 79 mg**

Top: Artichoke "Bowls."

Bottom: Velouté d'Escargot (Cream of Snail Soup), page 2.

Garden Patch Soup

1 pound very lean ground
  sirloin

4 ounces Canadian bacon,
  matchstick cut

1 medium onion, thinly sliced
  (2 cups)

½ cup thinly sliced celery

3 garlic cloves, minced or
  pressed

1 16-ounce can ready-cut
  tomatoes, undrained

1 8-ounce can tomato sauce (1
  cup)

2 cups water

1 16-ounce can red kidney
  beans, undrained

¾ teaspoon salt

1 teaspoon chili powder

⅛ teaspoon freshly ground
  black pepper

3 cups thinly shredded
  cabbage

Here is a "meal in minutes" that is inexpensive, easy to make, and will appeal to everyone in the family.

1. Cook the beef and bacon, stirring, until the beef is crumbly. Add the onion, celery, and garlic and cook 5 minutes. Stir in the remaining ingredients, except the cabbage, and bring to a simmer.

2. Add the cabbage and cook, covered, until the cabbage is tender, about 3 minutes.

Makes 10 cups; eight 1¼-cup servings

Each serving contains approximately:

Calories: 245   **Cholesterol: 45 mg**

Fat: 9 g   **Sodium: 953 mg**

Garden Patch Soup.

Tom Nuea Savoey

(Thai Beef Soup with Daikon Radish)

¾ *pound very lean beef, all visible fat removed, cubed*

5 cups water

1 12-ounce daikon (white radish), peeled and diced (3 cups)

1 tablespoon palm sugar or light brown sugar

3 tablespoons fish sauce or soy sauce

1 teaspoon chili paste

1 tablespoon rice vinegar

Cilantro (fresh coriander) leaves, for garnish

This is a very simple and beautifully balanced soup that I learned to make at The Thai Cooking School in the Oriental Hotel in Bangkok. Tom is the Thai word for "soup," nuea means "meat," and savoey means "fit for a king." The recipe came from the teacher's grandmother who made it for King Rama V of Thailand, and apparently he liked it. Palm sugar is available in all Asian markets.

1. Combine the beef and water in a heavy pan and bring to a boil. Reduce the heat and simmer, uncovered, for 15 minutes. Skim off any foam that may form on the surface.

2. Add the daikon and cook until the radish is translucent and can easily be pierced with a fork, about 10 minutes. Add all remaining ingredients, except the cilantro, and mix well. Serve in bowls or spooned over rice. Garnish with cilantro leaves.

Makes 6 cups; six 1-cup servings

Each serving contains approximately:

Calories: 120   **Cholesterol: 40 mg**

Fat: 5 g   **Sodium: 565 mg**

Black Bean Soup

8 ounces (1¼ cups) dried
  black beans, soaked
  overnight

4 cups defatted chicken stock

1 thick slice of lemon

1 medium onion, finely
  chopped (1½ cups)

2 garlic cloves, finely chopped
  (2 teaspoons)

2 teaspoons chili powder

¾ teaspoon ground cumin

½ jalapeño pepper, seeded
  and minced (2 teaspoons)

¼ cup chopped sun-dried
  tomatoes

¾ teaspoon salt (omit if using
  salted stock)

½ teaspoon dried oregano,
  crushed with a mortar and
  pestle

1 tablespoon sherry, or to taste

6 tablespoons light sour cream

1 tablespoon chopped fresh
  chives

Black Bean Soup is a little like chile in that everyone who makes it says, "Mine tastes best." Well, having created several recipes for this Cuban classic I can honestly say that I think mine tastes best!

1. Drain the beans and put them in a heavy pot. Add the stock and lemon slice and bring to a boil. Reduce the heat and simmer, covered, for 1 hour, or until the beans are tender.

2. While the beans are cooking, combine the onion, garlic, chili powder, cumin, and jalapeño and cook, covered, over very low heat until the onion is soft and translucent, about 10 to 15 minutes.

3. When the beans are tender, remove the lemon slice and add the onion mixture, sun-dried tomatoes, salt, and oregano, and cook for 15 more minutes. Remove 2 cups of the bean mixture and puree in a blender or food processor. Return the puree to the pot, add the sherry, and mix well.

4. To serve, ladle 1 cup of soup into each of six soup bowls. Garnish with 1 tablespoon sour cream and a sprinkling of chopped chives.

Makes 6 cups; six 1-cup servings

Each serving contains approximately:

Calories: 203   **Cholesterol: 6 mg**

Fat: 4 g   **Sodium: 380 mg**

Top: Black Bean Soup,
 page 7.

Right: Pasta e Fagioli
(Pasta and Bean Soup),
 page 10.

Split Pea Soup

1 medium onion, finely chopped (1½ cups)

3 stalks celery, without leaves, finely chopped (1½ cups)

1 cup finely chopped fresh parsley

1 garlic clove, minced or pressed

8 ounces Canadian bacon, diced

1 pound dried split peas, soaked overnight

8 cups defatted chicken stock

½ teaspoon salt (omit if using salted stock)

½ teaspoon freshly ground black pepper

Sherry (optional)

This recipe can be made either as written or with a ham hock. If using a ham hock, add it when you add the stock. After cooking the soup remove the ham hock and pick off the meat. Discard the bone and any fat, add the meat back into the soup, and refrigerate the soup for several hours or overnight. Then remove and discard the layer of fat that will have congealed on top of the soup and reheat your now defatted Split Pea Soup to the desired temperature.

1. Combine the onion, celery, parsley, garlic, and Canadian bacon in a large pot or soup kettle. Cook, covered, over low heat until soft, about 15 minutes. Stir occasionally and add a little water or stock, if necessary, to prevent scorching.

2. Drain the peas and add to the pot. Add the stock, salt, and pepper and bring to a boil. Reduce the heat and cook, covered, for 3 hours. If desired, add a little sherry to each serving.

Makes 12 cups; eight 1½-cup servings

Each serving contains approximately:

Calories: 260	**Cholesterol: 14 mg**
Fat: 3 g	**Sodium: 574 mg**

Split Pea Soup.

Pasta e Fagioli

(Pasta and Bean Soup)

1 medium onion, finely
  chopped (1½ cups)

3 garlic cloves, minced

1 pound fresh Roma tomatoes,
  peeled, seeded, and diced or
  1 16-ounce can plum
  tomatoes, drained and
  chopped

1 teaspoon dried oregano,
  crushed with a mortar and
  pestle

½ teaspoon dried thyme,
  crushed with a mortar and
  pestle

½ teaspoon dried rosemary,
  crushed with a mortar and
  pestle

¼ teaspoon dried marjoram,
  crushed with a mortar and
  pestle

⅛ teaspoon red pepper flakes

¼ teaspoon salt

¼ teaspoon freshly ground
  black pepper

1 15-ounce can cannellini,
  kidney, or navy beans,
  rinsed and drained

8 ounces rotelle pasta, cooked
  and drained

1 tablespoon extra-virgin
  olive oil

⅓ cup minced fresh parsley

½ teaspoon balsamic vinegar

¼ cup freshly grated
  Parmesan cheese

This is an adaptation of a recipe I learned to make at Ann Clark's cooking school, La Bonne Cuisine, in Austin, Texas. She does a weekend cooking class, called Ten Meals to Save Your Life, that is both a fun and a highly educational experience. As written, this recipe can also be served as a pasta entree. If you want your soup to be soupier, don't drain the canned tomatoes and increase the amount of water.

1. In a large skillet or 4- to 6-quart heavy casserole, cook the onion and garlic over low heat, covered, until the onion is soft and translucent, about 8 to 10 minutes. Add a little water, if necessary, to prevent scorching.

2. Add the tomatoes, oregano, thyme, rosemary, marjoram, red pepper flakes, salt, and pepper. Simmer until the sauce is thick and hot, about 10 minutes.

3. Add the rinsed and drained beans and ½ cup water and cook about 5 to 8 minutes to heat them through. Toss the cooked pasta with the olive oil and add to the soup along with the parsley and vinegar, stirring to mix well. To serve, spoon 1¼ cups soup into each of four bowls and top with 1 tablespoon freshly grated Parmesan cheese.

Makes 5 cups; four 1¼-cup servings

Each serving contains approximately:

Calories: 330	**Cholesterol: 4 mg**
Fat: 6 g	**Sodium: 610 mg**

Avgolemono

(Greek Lemon Soup)

3 ½ cups defatted chicken
  stock, or 2 14½-ounce cans
  sodium-reduced chicken
  broth

⅓ cup uncooked white rice

2 eggs

¼ cup fresh lemon juice

⅛ teaspoon freshly ground
  black pepper

I have always loved the flavor of this classic Greek soup but rarely order it in restaurants because it is so rich and so high in fat and cholesterol. I experimented with various recipes given to me by Greek friends and finally came up with this much lighter version which retains the integrity of the original despite a much better nutritional profile. Even my Greek friends are using my revised recipe.

1. Bring the stock to a boil in a heavy saucepan. Add the rice and simmer, covered, over low heat for 20 minutes or until the rice is tender.

2. While the rice is cooking, put the eggs in a bowl and whisk until well blended. When the rice is tender, spoon about 1 cup of the hot stock into the beaten eggs, a little at a time, stirring constantly. Pour the egg mixture back into the stock and rice mixture, stirring constantly. Add the lemon juice and pepper and mix well.

3. Serve immediately or refrigerate and serve cold. If you wish to reheat the soup, heat it just to serving temperature; do not boil.

Makes 4 cups; four 1-cup servings

Each serving contains approximately:

Calories: 125   **Cholesterol: 107 mg**

Fat: 4 g   **Sodium: 99 mg**

Tricolor Gazpacho

12 ounces (2 cups) red cherry tomatoes

12 ounces (2 cups) yellow cherry tomatoes

12 ounces (2 cups) small tomatillos, husks removed

2 green bell peppers, seeds and membranes removed and diced

1 medium sweet onion, diced

2 stalks celery, without leaves, diced (1 cup)

1 medium avocado, diced (1 cup)

2 garlic cloves, minced (2 teaspoons)

½ cup fresh lemon juice

1 tablespoon paprika

2 teaspoons salt

¼ teaspoon freshly ground black pepper

½ teaspoon Tabasco, or to taste

2 cups defatted beef stock

1 large cucumber, peeled, seeded, and diced (1½ cups)

Opposite: Avgolemono (Greek Lemon Soup), page 11.

Right: Tricolor Gazpacho.

The colorful combination of ingredients in this spicy southwestern soup makes it a perfect first course for a fiesta. If you can't find yellow tomatoes, use a yellow bell pepper for the color. For still more zing add a finely chopped jalapeño pepper.

1. Cut the tomatoes and tomatillos into quarters or halves, depending on their size. Combine them in a large bowl with the bell peppers, onion, celery, avocado, and garlic and mix well.

2. In another bowl, combine all remaining ingredients, except the cucumber, and mix well. Pour the stock mixture over the tomato mixture and again mix well. Cover and refrigerate for several hours before serving.

3. Just before serving, add the diced cucumber and mix well. Serve in chilled bowls.

Makes 10 cups; eight 1¼-cup servings

Each serving contains approximately:

Calories: 96	**Cholesterol: None**
Fat: 5 g	**Sodium: 662 mg**

Chilled English
Stilton-Pear Soup

*1 medium onion, finely
chopped (1½ cups)*

*1 leek, white part only, finely
chopped (2 cups)*

*2 stalks celery, without leaves,
thinly sliced (1 cup)*

4 cups defatted chicken stock

*1 cup (4 ounces) grated
fat-reduced Monterey Jack
cheese*

1½ cups 2% low-fat milk

*½ cup (2 ounces) crumbled
Stilton cheese*

*½ cup (2 ounces) low-fat
cottage cheese*

*3 pears, peeled, cored, and
diced*

*If you've been searching for a truly unique first course—or even a
rather bizarre dessert—this delicious and unusual cold cheese and
fruit soup may be the perfect answer. I have yet to serve it to anyone
who hasn't asked for the recipe.*

1. In a heavy pot combine the onion, leek, and celery and cook,
covered, over low heat until soft, about 15 minutes. Stir occasionally and add a little stock, if necessary, to prevent scorching. Add
the stock, mix well, and simmer for 20 minutes. Remove from the
heat and allow to cool slightly, then pour the mixture into a blender
and puree. Pour through a sieve or strainer, pressing through with
the back of a spoon.

2. Return the strained mixture to the pot and reheat to a simmer.
Add the Jack cheese and stir until completely melted. Remove
from the heat and when the soup reaches room temperature add
the milk, Stilton and cottage cheeses, and the pears. Refrigerate
until cold before serving.

Makes 6 cups; six 1-cup servings

Each serving contains approximately:

Calories: 242   **Cholesterol: 27 mg**

Fat: 10 g   **Sodium: 423 mg**

Catalina Clam Chowder

2 medium onions, diced
  (3 cups)

6 ounces Canadian bacon,
  diced (1½ cups)

2 teaspoons chili powder

1 teaspoon salt

¾ teaspoon dried oregano,
  crushed with a mortar and
  pestle

¼ teaspoon freshly ground
  black pepper

Dash of red pepper flakes

1 16-ounce can crushed or
  ready-cut tomatoes

6 cups water

3 medium potatoes (1 pound),
  peeled and diced (3 cups)

2 10-ounce cans baby clams,
  drained

1 12½-ounce can evaporated
  skim milk

1 teaspoon balsamic vinegar

2 slices whole wheat bread,
  toasted and ground into fine
  crumbs (½ cup)

When I was growing up we frequently went to Catalina Island, a small island off the southern California coast, for weekends. It was difficult to buy ingredients at the tiny yacht harbor market so we developed recipes for dishes that could be made primarily with canned products and ingredients that stored well. This Catalina Clam Chowder was always a hit.

1. Combine the onions and bacon in a heavy pot or soup kettle and cook, covered, over low heat until the onions are soft and translucent. Add the chili powder, salt, oregano, pepper, red pepper flakes, and tomatoes and mix well. Add the water and bring to a boil. Reduce the heat and simmer, uncovered, for 45 minutes.

2. Add the potatoes and cook until the potatoes are tender, about 10 to 15 minutes.

3. Add the clams, milk, vinegar, and bread crumbs and mix well. Do not allow to boil after adding the clams or they will become tough.

Makes 10 cups; eight 1¼-cup servings

Each serving contains approximately:

Calories: 250   **Cholesterol: 50 mg**

Fat: 3 g   **Sodium: 853 mg**

Yaam Ma Khuea Yow (Herbed Eggplant Salad), page 30.

Celery Root Salad

Pasta Pesto Salad

Light Pesto Sauce

salads

Tropical Slaw

Salade Niçoise

Hot German Potato Salad

Wilted Watercress Salad

A-Jaad
(Thai Cucumber Salad)

Caponata
(Eggplant Appetizer)

Antipasto Salad

Yaam Ma Khuea Yow
(Herbed Eggplant Salad)

Turkey and Winter Fruit Salad

Celery Root Salad

1½ cups (12 ounces) silken soft tofu

3 tablespoons fresh lemon juice

3 tablespoons extra-virgin olive oil

3 tablespoons Dijon mustard

¾ teaspoon salt

¼ teaspoon freshly ground black pepper, or to taste

1 pound celery root, peeled and grated (5 cups)

What we call celery root is not the subterranean portion of common celery, but rather the root of the celeriac plant, which has a subtle but distinctive flavor and is good both raw and cooked. The mustardy taste of this salad is typical of the celery root salads served in bistros throughout France.

1. Combine all ingredients, except the celery root, in a blender container and blend until satin smooth.

2. Combine the dressing and celery root and mix well. Cover and allow to stand several hours or overnight before serving.

Makes 4 cups; eight ½-cup servings

Each serving contains approximately:

Calories: 107   **Cholesterol: None**

Fat: 8 g   **Sodium: 359 mg**

Pasta Pesto Salad

2 quarts florets and julienne-cut fresh vegetables (use a colorful assortment: broccoli, cauliflower, carrots, zucchini, yellow squash, etc.)

1 pound cooked rotini pasta (al dente) (8 cups)

1 ½ cups Light Pesto Sauce (page 20)

2 cups peeled and diced Roma tomatoes

½ cup (2 ounces) grated Parmesan cheese

8 teaspoons pine nuts, toasted in a 350°F. oven 8 to 10 minutes

8 sprigs fresh basil, for garnish

This delicious country Italian salad is usually served cold or at room temperature. However, I sometimes serve it hot and call it Pasta Pesto Primavera.

1. Steam the vegetables, separately, until crisp tender. Rinse with cold water to hold their color.

2. Combine the cooked vegetables, pasta, and Light Pesto Sauce and toss thoroughly.

3. To serve, mound 2 cups pasta salad on a plate, sprinkle with ¼ cup diced tomatoes and 1 tablespoon Parmesan cheese, then top with 1 teaspoon toasted pine nuts. Garnish with a basil sprig.

Makes eight 2-cup servings

Each serving contains approximately:

Calories: 475   **Cholesterol: 12 mg**

Fat: 23 g   **Sodium: 402 mg**

Light Pesto Sauce

Celery Root Salad, page 18.

¼ *cup pine nuts, toasted in a 350°F. oven 8 to 10 minutes*

2 cups packed fresh basil, all stems removed

2 cups packed fresh spinach, stems removed and deveined

4 garlic cloves (4 teaspoons)

1 cup (4 ounces) grated Parmesan cheese

½ *teaspoon fresh lemon juice*

¼ *teaspoon salt*

¼ *teaspoon freshly ground black pepper*

½ *cup extra-virgin olive oil*

Pasta Pesto Salad, page 19.

1. Combine all ingredients in a food processor fitted with the metal blade. Mix until a smooth paste is formed.

2. Refrigerate in a tightly covered container or freeze in containers of an appropriate size.

Makes 1½ cups; eight 3-tablespoon servings

Each serving contains approximately:

Calories: 181   **Cholesterol: 7 mg**

Fat: 18 g   **Sodium: 262 mg**

Hot German Potato Salad, page 23.

Tropical Slaw

¼ cup walnuts, chopped

1 20-ounce can juice-packed crushed pineapple, including juice

1 ½ teaspoons coconut extract

1 head raw cauliflower, finely grated (about 4 cups; you can do this in the food processor)

1 cup seedless red grapes, quartered

This salad is a great impostor. By combining the grated raw cauliflower with the coconut extract and allowing it time to marinate for several hours, the cauliflower absorbs the coconut flavor and the perception is that you are eating a grated coconut and pineapple salad. I call for red grapes in this recipe strictly for color. Green grapes can certainly be substituted if red ones are not available.

1. Toast the walnuts in a preheated 350°F. oven until golden brown, about 8 to 10 minutes. Watch carefully because they burn easily. Set aside.

2. Pour the juice off the pineapple into a large bowl and set the crushed pineapple aside. Add the coconut extract to the juice and mix well. Add the cauliflower and mix well; add the crushed pineapple and mix well again. Cover and refrigerate for at least 2 hours before serving. (It is even better if allowed to stand several hours or overnight.)

3. To serve, add the grapes and mix well. Divide evenly onto chilled plates and lightly sprinkle each serving with ½ teaspoon toasted walnuts.

Makes 4 cups; eight ½-cup servings

Each serving contains approximately:

Calories: 89   **Cholesterol: None**

Fat: 2 g   **Sodium: 9 mg**

Tropical Slaw.

Salade Niçoise

vinaigrette:

¼ cup red wine vinegar

½ teaspoon salt

¼ teaspoon freshly ground
   black pepper

¼ cup water

¼ cup extra-virgin olive oil

2 tablespoons capers, drained

salad:

½ pound fresh tuna or 1
   7-ounce can water-packed
   albacore, drained

8 small new potatoes,
   unpeeled, cooked, and sliced

2 red bell peppers, roasted,
   peeled, seeded, and sliced in
   1-inch strips (see page 73)

½ pound thin green beans,
   cooked until just tender

½ large red onion, very thinly
   sliced

8 anchovy fillets, rinsed and
   dried

4 small tomatoes, cut in
   wedges

4 hard-boiled eggs, whites
   only, halved

4 large sprigs fresh rosemary
   or thyme, for garnish
   (optional)

This salad is classically made with canned tuna but I like it even better with grilled fresh fish. A great variation on this recipe is to omit the potatoes and put all of the other ingredients on a piece of crusty French bread for a Sandwich Niçoise.

1. Combine the vinegar and salt and mix until the salt is dissolved. Add all other vinaigrette ingredients and mix well. (If possible, make the day before serving.)

2. Marinate the raw tuna or drained canned tuna for 1 hour in 2 tablespoons of the vinaigrette. If using raw tuna, grill until medium rare.

3. Arrange the salad ingredients, side by side, in an attractive manner on a large white platter; do not toss. Just before serving, pour the vinaigrette over the salad and garnish with sprigs of rosemary or thyme, if desired.

Makes 4 servings

Each serving contains approximately:

Calories: 345   **Cholesterol: 36 mg**

Fat: 17 g   **Sodium: 500 mg**

Hot German Potato Salad

4 medium baking potatoes
  (2 pounds)

4 slices Canadian bacon
  (4 ounces), diced

1 tablespoon canola oil

1 medium onion, finely chopped
  (1½ cups)

½ teaspoon salt

¼ teaspoon freshly ground
  black pepper

¼ cup cider vinegar

2 tablespoons sugar

¼ teaspoon liquid smoke

Parsley, for garnish (optional)

I usually serve this salad as a side dish with grilled poultry or meat. If there are leftovers, I dice up cooked meat, toss it in the salad, and serve it cold for lunch the next day.

1. Preheat the oven to 400°F. Wash the potatoes well and dry thoroughly. Pierce with the tines of a fork to keep skins from bursting. Bake for 1 hour. Remove from the oven and allow to cool until safe to handle. Dice the potatoes and set them aside in a large bowl.

2. In a nonstick skillet, cook the bacon until lightly browned. Remove it from the skillet and add it to the potatoes. Do not wash the skillet.

3. In the same skillet, heat the oil. Add the onion and cook over medium-high heat, until lightly browned. Add all other ingredients, except the parsley, and mix well. Add the onion mixture to the potatoes and bacon and mix well. Garnish with parsley, if desired, and serve warm.

Makes 6 cups; eight ¾-cup servings

Each serving contains approximately:

Calories: 171   **Cholesterol: 7 mg**

Fat: 3 g   **Sodium: 357 mg**

Wilted Watercress Salad

4 bunches watercress (1 pound), stems removed (8 cups)

2 tomatoes, peeled, seeded, and diced (1 cup)

2 tablespoons extra-virgin olive oil

2 garlic cloves, minced or pressed

2 cups thinly sliced fresh mushrooms (½ pound)

2 tablespoons fresh lemon juice

½ teaspoon salt

¼ teaspoon freshly ground black pepper

The clean, fresh taste of this salad combined with the slightly bitter bite of the watercress gives it a refreshingly different flavor. I like it so much that I often add julienne-cut cooked chicken breast and serve it as a luncheon entree.

1. In a large bowl, combine the watercress and diced tomatoes and mix well. Set aside.

2. In a saucepan, combine 1 tablespoon of the oil and the garlic. Heat the oil over medium-high heat just until the garlic sizzles. Add the mushrooms and cook, covered, until soft.

3. Combine the lemon juice, salt, pepper, and remaining tablespoon of oil and mix well. Add to the mushrooms, mix well, and pour over the watercress and tomatoes. Toss lightly and serve immediately, while still warm.

Makes 8 cups; eight 1-cup servings

Each serving contains approximately:

Calories: 45   **Cholesterol: None**

Fat: 4 g   **Sodium: 165 mg**

Top: A-Jaad (Thai Cucumber Salad), page 26.

Bottom: Wilted Watercress Salad, opposite.

A-Jaad

(Thai Cucumber Salad)

½ cup rice vinegar

2 tablespoons sugar

1 teaspoon salt

2 tablespoons chopped red
   chilies, or to taste (see Note)

½ cup sliced shallots

2 cups sliced cucumbers

2 tablespoons chopped peanuts
   (optional)

2 tablespoons chopped cilantro
   (fresh coriander) leaves
   (optional)

Green onion, for garnish
   (optional)

In Thailand this spicy salad is served as a side dish with almost everything.

1. Combine the vinegar, sugar, and salt in a saucepan. Cook over low heat, stirring constantly, until the sugar and salt are completely dissolved. Remove from the heat and cool to room temperature.

2. Combine the vinegar mixture with the chilies, shallots, and cucumbers, and mix well. Serve immediately or the cucumber will become soft. Sprinkle with peanuts and/or cilantro, and garnish with a green onion, if desired.

Makes 2 cups; four ½-cup servings

Each serving contains approximately:

Calories: 52	Cholesterol: None
Fat: Negligible	Sodium: 596 mg

Variation: *Malaysian Cucumber Salad:* Omit the peanuts and cilantro and add 1 cup of finely diced fresh pineapple.

Each variation serving contains approximately:

Calories: 71	Cholesterol: None
Fat: Negligible	Sodium: 597 mg

Note: For a milder salad, use red bell pepper in place of hot chilies.

Caponata

(Eggplant Appetizer)

1 tablespoon extra-virgin olive oil

½ cup minced onion

1 medium eggplant, unpeeled and cut into 1-inch cubes

1 cup tomato sauce

1 teaspoon anchovy paste

1 teaspoon salt

2 tablespoons capers, drained and rinsed

3 tablespoons red wine vinegar

1 cup water

½ teaspoon dried basil, crushed with a mortar and pestle

1 tablespoon sugar

1. Heat the oil in a heavy skillet. Add the onion and cook, covered, over medium-low heat until soft and translucent, about 10 minutes. Remove the onion from the pan and set aside.

2. In the same skillet over medium-high heat, cook the eggplant, stirring frequently, for 10 minutes. Return the onion to the pan and add the remaining ingredients. Reduce the heat to low and simmer, uncovered, for 30 minutes. Allow to cool to room temperature and store, covered, in the refrigerator.

Makes 3 cups; four ¾-cup servings

Each serving contains approximately:

Calories: 90   **Cholesterol: 3 mg**

Fat: 4 g   **Sodium: 1140 mg**

Antipasto Salad

dressing:

½ teaspoon balsamic vinegar

¼ teaspoon salt

1 tablespoon dry red wine

⅛ teaspoon dry mustard

¼ teaspoon sugar

Dash of freshly ground black
  pepper

⅛ teaspoon dried basil,
  crushed with a mortar and
  pestle

⅛ teaspoon dried tarragon,
  crushed with a mortar and
  pestle

⅛ teaspoon dried oregano,
  crushed with a mortar and
  pestle

2 tablespoons extra-virgin
  olive oil

salad:

1 ounce (¼ cup packed) sun-
  dried tomatoes

8 cups assorted salad greens,
  torn in bite-size pieces

¼ cup (1 ounce) freshly grated
  Parmesan cheese

¾ cup Caponata (Eggplant
  Appetizer), page 27

¾ cup cooked garbanzo beans
  (chick-peas)

½ cup (2 ounces) diced
  part-skim mozzarella cheese

Edible flowers for garnish,
  optional

This lush-looking and tasty salad is one of my favorite summer supper entrees. Here I've garnished it with nasturtiums from my own garden. All you need to serve with this salad is a loaf of crusty Italian bread.

1. Combine the vinegar and salt and stir until the salt is dissolved. Add all the other dressing ingredients except the oil and mix thoroughly. Slowly add the oil, stirring constantly. Set aside.

2. Using scissors or kitchen shears cut the tomatoes into thin strips and put them in a small bowl. Cover with boiling water and allow to stand for 2 minutes. Drain and set aside.

3. Toss the salad greens with the Parmesan cheese. Add the drained tomatoes and all the remaining salad ingredients and mix well. Add the dressing and toss thoroughly.

Makes about 9 cups; six 1½-cup servings

Each serving contains approximately:

Calories: 229   **Cholesterol: 12 mg**

Antipasto Salad.

Yaam Ma Khuea Yow

(Herbed Eggplant Salad)

1 large or 3 small eggplant

1 teaspoon red chili paste

3 tablespoons fresh lime juice

3 tablespoons fish sauce

2 tablespoons brine from pickled garlic

½ cup pulverized dried shrimp

2 tablespoons finely chopped pickled garlic

2 tablespoons finely chopped garlic (6 cloves)

3 tablespoons finely chopped shallots

1 tablespoon finely chopped cilantro root or stems

Chopped hard-boiled egg whites, for garnish (optional)

Cilantro (fresh coriander) leaves, for garnish (optional)

Chilies, for garnish (optional)

Eggplant is one of the mainstays of Thai cooking and there are more varieties and sizes available in Thailand than I have seen anywhere else in the world. For this recipe you can use either large eggplant or the small Japanese variety. Chili paste, fish sauce, pickled garlic, and dried shrimp are all available in Thai or Asian markets.

1. Preheat the oven to 300°F. Cut the eggplant in half lengthwise, and place cut side down on a baking sheet that has been sprayed with nonstick vegetable coating. Bake it until it can be easily pierced with a fork, about 15 to 20 minutes. Do not overcook or the eggplant will get mushy. When the eggplant is cool enough to be handled safely, carefully remove and discard the skin, then place the flesh in the refrigerator until cold.

2. Cube the cold eggplant (you should have about 3 cups) and place it in a large mixing bowl. Combine the chili paste, lime juice, fish sauce, and brine from the pickled garlic, mixing well. Pour the mixture over the eggplant and toss to distribute evenly.

3. In another bowl, combine the shrimp, pickled garlic, garlic, shallots, and cilantro and mix well. Combine this mixture with the eggplant and mix well. Cover and refrigerate until chilled before serving.

4. To serve, garnish each serving with chopped egg whites, cilantro, and chilies, if desired.

Makes 4 cups; four 1-cup servings

Each serving contains approximately:

Calories: 110	**Cholesterol: 76 mg**
Fat: 2 g	**Sodium: 871 mg**

Turkey and Winter Fruit Salad

½ cup chopped raw almonds

¼ cup rice vinegar

1 garlic clove, minced or pressed

2 teaspoons sodium-reduced soy sauce

4 teaspoons packed dark brown sugar

1 teaspoon curry powder

2 tablespoons canola oil

8 cups washed mixed greens, torn in bite-size pieces

2 large navel oranges (1 pound), peeled and diced (2 cups)

2 medium red Delicious apples (12 ounces), diced (2 cups)

1 pound julienne-cut cooked turkey breast

2 tablespoons chopped chives, for garnish

I originally developed this salad to use up the turkey I had left over after Thanksgiving and Christmas when the only really good seasonal fruits available are apples and oranges. I still call it Winter Fruit Salad, which sounds much snappier than Holiday Leftover Salad.

1. Toast the almonds in a preheated 350°F. oven until lightly browned, 8 to 10 minutes. Watch carefully because they burn easily. Set aside.

2. Combine the vinegar, garlic, soy sauce, brown sugar, and curry powder and whisk until well blended. Slowly whisk in the oil. Set aside.

3. Combine the greens, oranges, apples, and turkey. Pour the dressing over the top and gently toss the salad until it is well coated with dressing.

4. To serve, place 1½ cups salad on each of eight plates. Top each serving with 1 tablespoon toasted almonds and a sprinkle of chopped chives for garnish.

Makes 12 cups; eight 1½-cup servings

Each serving contains approximately:

Calories: 237

Fat: 10 g

Cholesterol: 39 mg

Sodium: 91 mg

Tuscan Oven-baked Potatoes, page 34.

Tuscan Oven-baked Potatoes

Mediterranean Grilled Vegetables

vege-

Herbed Onion Rings

Overnight Baked Beans

tables

Indian Corn Casserole

Hummis

French Gardener's Stew

Roasted Garlic

Tuscan Oven-baked Potatoes

2 pounds small new potatoes

1 tablespoon corn oil margarine

1 tablespoon extra-virgin olive oil

12 garlic cloves, peeled

Several sprigs of fresh rosemary, or 1 tablespoon dried rosemary, crushed with a mortar and pestle

I learned to make these potatoes, smothered in garlic and rosemary, at Badia a Coltibuono, Lorenza de Medici's picturesque villa and cooking school in Tuscany. I particularly like them with grilled vegetables, poultry, or meat—or a combination of all three.

1. Preheat the oven to 400°F. Scrub the potatoes completely clean and slice, unpeeled, into halves.

2. Heat the margarine and oil in a large skillet. Add the potatoes and garlic and stir over medium heat until well coated.

3. Spray a baking sheet with nonstick vegetable coating. Spread the potatoes evenly on the sheet and top with the rosemary. Bake until a deep golden brown, about 45 to 55 minutes, stirring occasionally to assure the potatoes brown evenly.

Makes 4 cups; eight ½-cup servings

Each serving contains approximately:

Calories: 140   **Cholesterol: None**

Fat: 3 g   **Sodium: 30 mg**

Mediterranean Grilled Vegetables

Extra-virgin olive oil

Blend to taste:

  Fresh parsley, minced
  Fresh sage, minced
  Fresh thyme, minced
  Fresh rosemary, minced
  Fresh oregano, minced
  Fresh basil, minced

Eggplant, thinly sliced, salted, rinsed, and drained

Red, green, and yellow bell peppers, seeded, membranes removed, roasted, and peeled (see page 73)

Zucchini, thinly sliced lengthwise

Onion, blanched and thinly sliced

Artichoke bottoms, blanched and thinly sliced

Fennel, thinly sliced lengthwise

Garlic cloves

It's a fact of life that some vegetables take longer to cook than others. Some cooks start the long-cooking ones early, or the short-cooking ones late, but my solution to this problem is to blanch the vegetables that require a longer grilling time. Also, I salt the eggplant and allow it to stand for at least 45 minutes and then rinse it thoroughly before grilling it. This takes out the bitterness often found in eggplant.

1. Combine the olive oil and the herbs of your choice and allow to stand several hours or overnight. Prepare the coals; they should be glowing red, but not flaming.

2. Brush the vegetables with the herbed olive oil and grill until lightly browned on both sides. Cooking times will vary greatly depending on the type of vegetable, the heat of the coals, and the distance from the fire.

3. Serve with a ramekin of herbed olive oil and thinly sliced bread, if desired.

Each serving contains approximately:

Calories: Varies   **Cholesterol: None**

Fat: Negligible   **Sodium: Varies**

Herbed Onion Rings

2 large onions, cut
   horizontally and separated
   into rings

2 egg whites, lightly beaten

1 cup whole wheat flour

½ teaspoon salt

1 teaspoon dried herbs (thyme,
   oregano, tarragon, etc.),
   crushed with a mortar and
   pestle

Herbed Onion Rings.

Gone are the days when onion rings mean deep-frying oil splattered everywhere. These "oven-fried" Herbed Onion Rings are sensational, easy to make, and don't mess up your kitchen. Do serve them immediately because just like any onion ring the moisture of the onions will cause them to lose their crispness quickly.

1. Preheat the oven to 400°F. Steam the onion rings over rapidly boiling water for 3 minutes. Rinse with cold water to stop the cooking and drain well.

2. Combine the onion rings with the egg whites in a large bowl and mix well to coat evenly.

3. Cover a baking sheet with parchment paper or generously spray the baking sheet with nonstick vegetable coating. Combine the flour, salt, and herbs in a paper bag and shake to mix well. Put the onion rings, *one at a time*, into the bag and shake well to coat thoroughly. Place the onion rings on the baking sheet, being careful not to overlap them.

4. Generously spray the onion rings with nonstick vegetable coating and bake in the preheated oven for 15 minutes. Turn the rings over with a fork or tongs, spray them again with the nonstick coating and return to the oven for 10 more minutes.

Makes eight ¼-cup servings

Each serving contains approximately:

Calories: 70   **Cholesterol: None**

Fat: Negligible   **Sodium: 162 mg**

Opposite: French Gardener's Stew, page 42.

Overnight Baked Beans

1 pound (2½ cups) dried small white beans, soaked several hours or overnight

1 medium onion, minced

1 garlic clove, minced or pressed

1 8-ounce can tomato sauce

1 cup frozen unsweetened apple juice concentrate, undiluted, thawed

2 tablespoons spicy brown mustard

2 tablespoons dark molasses

1 tablespoon Worcestershire sauce

1 teaspoon salt

½ teaspoon freshly ground black pepper

By using very low heat for a very long time, this cooking technique allows the beans to absorb the sauce and therefore intensifies the flavor of the dish. It also produces a thick, almost candied, texture which seems decadently rich. Actually these baked beans are very low in fat and extremely high in fiber. Of course, these Overnight Baked Beans can be baked all day instead with equally good results.

1. Drain the beans and rinse thoroughly. Place them in a large pot and cover with at least 2 inches of cold water. Bring to a boil, remove any foam that appears on the top, and reduce the heat to low. Simmer, covered, until the beans are tender, about 2 hours. Drain and set aside.

2. Preheat the oven to 250°F. Cook the onion, covered, in a heavy skillet over low heat until soft, about 10 minutes. Stir occasionally and add a little water or stock, if necessary, to prevent scorching. Add the remaining ingredients and mix well. Add the beans and again mix well.

3. Spoon the mixture into a 2-quart baking dish or bean pot and bake, covered, in the preheated oven for 6 to 8 hours.

Makes 6 cups; twelve ½-cup servings

Each serving contains approximately:

Calories: 190	Cholesterol: None
Fat: 1 g	Sodium: 374 mg

Indian Corn Casserole

6 ears fresh corn in the husks

½ cup minced onion

1½ cups grated zucchini
(2 medium, 10 ounces) (You
can do this in the food
processor.)

¼ cup chopped, canned green
chilies

¼ cup water

¼ cup whole wheat flour

½ teaspoon salt

¼ teaspoon freshly ground
black pepper

⅛ teaspoon cayenne pepper

½ teaspoon ground cumin

½ teaspoon chili powder

1½ cups cooked beans, pinto,
small white, or black
(15½-ounce can, drained)

Corn, beans, and squash, the Indians' "Inseparable Sisters," are combined in this tasty casserole. Baking it in the corn husks gives the dish an added roasted corn flavor and also provides a perfect presentation.

1. Preheat the oven to 325°F. Remove and discard the tough outer husks from each ear of corn. Reserve the inner husks to line the baking dish. Carefully remove all the silk. Grate the corn using the large-hole side of the grater. Press the ear firmly against the grater to squeeze out all the "milk" from the cob. Set the grated corn aside. Discard the cobs.

2. Blanch the reserved corn husks in boiling water. Rinse in cool water and drape each husk out flat over the side of a large bowl.

3. Combine the onion, zucchini, chilies, and water in a skillet or saucepan. Cook, covered, over low heat until the onion is soft and translucent, 8 to 10 minutes.

4. While the onion mixture is cooking combine the flour, salt, black pepper, cayenne pepper, cumin, and chili powder, stirring to mix well. Add it to the cooked onion and stir until well mixed. Add the grated corn and the beans, stir, and bring to a simmer. Continue to simmer for 5 minutes, stirring frequently.

5. Line the bottom of a 1-quart baking dish with half the corn husks. Spoon the corn mixture on top of the corn husks and carefully spread it evenly over the bottom. Cover the top with the remaining corn husks. Bake for 25 minutes in the preheated oven.

6. To serve, remove the corn husks from the top. Place 2 husks on each plate and mound 1 cup of the baked mixture on top.

Makes 4 cups; four 1-cup servings

Each serving contains approximately:

Calories: 204   **Cholesterol: None**

Fat: 2 g   **Sodium: 415 mg**

Hummis

½ pound dried garbanzo beans (chick-peas), soaked several hours or overnight (see Note)

6 cups water

1¾ teaspoons salt

4 garlic cloves, chopped

¼ cup fresh lemon juice

3 tablespoons dark sesame oil

⅛ teaspoon freshly ground black pepper

⅛ teaspoon cayenne pepper

This tasty, Middle Eastern mixture can be used as a spread, a dip, or a sauce. I like it best spread on pita bread and as a sauce on poultry.

1. Drain the beans and rinse thoroughly. Combine the beans, water, and 1 teaspoon of the salt in a pot and bring to a boil. Reduce the heat and simmer, covered, for 1 hour. Drain the beans, reserving the cooking water.

2. Place the drained beans in a food processor. Add all other ingredients and blend until smooth. Add enough of the cooking water for the mixture to be the consistency of creamy peanut butter. Serve with pita bread, if desired.

Makes 3 cups; twelve ¼-cup servings

Each serving contains approximately:

Calories: 102   **Cholesterol: None**

Fat: 5 g   **Sodium: 350 mg**

Note: For faster hummis, use 2 16-ounce cans of garbanzo beans. Drain the beans and use the liquid from the can to obtain the correct consistency when processing the hummis. When using canned beans omit the salt from the recipe.

Hummis.

French Gardener's Stew

beans:

$\frac{1}{2}$ cup dried small white beans,
  soaked overnight and
  drained

1 onion, peeled and stuck with
  2 cloves

1 carrot, peeled and quartered

$\frac{1}{2}$ teaspoon salt

$\frac{1}{4}$ teaspoon freshly ground
  black pepper

$\frac{1}{2}$ teaspoon dried thyme,
  crushed with a mortar and
  pestle

$\frac{1}{2}$ teaspoon dried rosemary,
  crushed with a mortar and
  pestle

vegetables:

2 medium turnips, peeled and
  cut in 1-inch cubes

2 medium potatoes, peeled and
  cut in 1-inch cubes

2 stalks celery, without leaves,
  sliced into $\frac{1}{4}$-inch crescents

3 large carrots, peeled and
  sliced in $\frac{1}{2}$-inch rounds

4 leeks, white part only, sliced
  in $\frac{1}{2}$-inch rounds and rinsed
  thoroughly

$\frac{1}{4}$ head medium cabbage,
  shredded

5 cups water

1 teaspoon salt

This savory combination of vegetables, beans, and herbs is made with ingredients that are readily available most of the year. It is easy to make, inexpensive, and sure to please even the most discriminating palate.

1. Combine all bean ingredients in a medium pot, cover with water, and bring to a boil. Reduce the heat to simmer and cook until the beans are tender, about 2 hours. Drain the beans and discard the carrot and onion.

2. While the beans are cooking, combine the turnips, potatoes, celery, carrots, leeks, and cabbage with 1 cup of the water in a large pot or soup kettle. Cook, covered, over low heat until the vegetables are tender, about 30 minutes. *Do not brown.*

3. Add the drained beans to the vegetables. Add the remaining 4 cups of water, salt, pepper, thyme, and rosemary. Bring to a boil, then reduce the heat and simmer, covered, for 30 minutes. Remove from the heat and allow to cool slightly. Remove 4 cups of the vegetables and puree. Pour the pureed vegetables back into the stew and mix well. Heat to the desired temperature.

¼ teaspoon freshly ground black
  pepper

1 teaspoon dried thyme, crushed
  with a mortar and pestle

1 teaspoon dried rosemary,
  crushed with a mortar and
  pestle

Finely chopped fresh parsley,
  for garnish (optional)

4. To serve, ladle 1½ cups soup into a bowl or soup plate. Top with chopped parsley, if desired. I like to top each serving with Light Aïoli (page 81) or freshly grated Parmesan cheese.

Makes 12 cups; eight 1½-cup servings

Each serving contains approximately:

Calories: 131   **Cholesterol: None**

Fat: 5 g   **Sodium: 515 mg**

Roasted Garlic

Heads of whole garlic

Extra-virgin olive oil, for
  drizzling

This creamy and aromatic spread is a great substitute for butter and oils. It's very low calorie, fat-free, and contains no cholesterol. Try it on baked potatoes and as a spread for bread.

1. Preheat the oven to 350°F. Select large-cloved heads of garlic. Slice the top off each head of garlic and place it, cut side up, in a baking dish or pan. Drizzle the top of each head with a few drops of olive oil.

2. Cover the pan with aluminum foil and bake, covered, for 30 minutes. Remove the foil and continue to bake 15 to 30 minutes more until the garlic is soft and a spreadable consistency when squeezed from the skins. Spread on your favorite crusty bread.

Each tablespoon spread contains approximately:

Calories: 6   **Cholesterol: None**

Fat: Negligible   **Sodium: 1 mg**

Barley and Currant Pilaf, page 47.

Spicy Carrot Risotto

Barley and Currant Pilaf

Halloween Pasta

Macronade on Rigatoni

grains & pasta

Thai Peanut Rice

Pasta alla Checca

Macaroni and Cheese

Pad Thai
(Stir-fried Noodles, Thai Style)

Pastitsio

Pacific Rim Pizza Quiche

Spicy Carrot Risotto

1 tablespoon extra-virgin
    olive oil

½ cup finely chopped onion

½ cup Arborio rice

1 garlic clove, minced or
    pressed

¼ cup dry sherry

1 cup defatted chicken stock or
    water

2 cups carrot juice

¼ teaspoon salt (omit if using
    salted stock)

¼ teaspoon ground cinnamon

¼ teaspoon ground cumin

⅛ teaspoon ground nutmeg

Dash of cayenne pepper

1 tablespoon corn oil
    margarine

¼ cup freshly grated
    Parmesan cheese

Chives, for garnish (optional)

Julienne-cut red onion, for
    garnish (optional)

Grated Parmesan cheese, for
    garnish (optional)

When I first saw this brilliant orange risotto I was enchanted with the vibrancy of the color. The minute I tasted it I knew I had to have the recipe to share with my readers. The dish was created by the talented young chef Matthew Kenney for the New York restaurant Alo Alo.

1. Heat the olive oil in a heavy pan. Add the onion and cook over low heat until soft and translucent, 8 to 10 minutes. Add the rice and garlic and cook, stirring constantly, for 2 minutes to coat the rice with oil.

2. Add the sherry and cook until the rice is almost dry. Add the stock or water and again cook until the rice is almost dry.

3. Lower the heat to simmer and begin adding the carrot juice, ½ cup at a time, simmering until the rice becomes almost dry but always leaving a veil of liquid over the top before adding more juice. Stir frequently. When adding the last ½ cup carrot juice, add the salt, cinnamon, cumin, nutmeg, and cayenne. Cook until most of the liquid is absorbed and stir in the margarine.

4. Remove from the heat, stir in the Parmesan cheese, and serve immediately. Garnish as desired.

Makes 3 cups; six ½-cup servings
Each serving contains approximately:

Calories: 150   **Cholesterol: 3 mg**

Fat: 6 g   **Sodium: 204 mg**

Barley and Currant Pilaf

¾ cup pearl barley

1 teaspoon canola or corn oil

½ medium onion, finely
  chopped (¾ cup)

1 small carrot, peeled and
  finely chopped (½ cup)

1 stalk celery, without leaves,
  finely chopped (½ cup)

1 teaspoon dried sage, crushed
  with a mortar and pestle

1 teaspoon dried thyme, crushed
  with a mortar and pestle

1 bay leaf

½ teaspoon salt (omit if using
  salted stock)

¼ teaspoon freshly ground
  black pepper

½ cup currants

2 cups defatted turkey or
  chicken stock

This pilaf is excellent served with turkey at holiday meals in place of the more traditional dressings and stuffings. It is also good combined with cooked, diced turkey or beans for an unusual one-dish meal.

1. Place the barley in a heavy skillet over low heat and, stirring frequently, cook until lightly browned, about 20 minutes. Put the browned barley in a bowl and set aside.

2. Place the pan back on the stove and heat the oil. Add the onion, carrot, and celery. Cook, covered, over low heat until the onion is soft, about 8 to 10 minutes.

3. Add the barley, seasonings, and currants and mix well. Add the stock and bring to a boil. Reduce the heat, cover, and simmer until the barley is tender and all the liquid is absorbed, about 35 minutes. Add more stock if the barley starts to get too dry before it is tender. Remove the bay leaf before serving.

Makes 4 cups; eight ½-cup servings

Each serving contains approximately:

Calories: 116	**Cholesterol: Negligible**
Fat: 2 g	**Sodium: 179 mg**

Halloween Pasta

1 medium onion, finely
chopped (1½ cups)

2 tablespoons water

1½ tablespoons marjoram,
crushed with a mortar and
pestle

1 teaspoon salt

¼ teaspoon freshly ground
white pepper

¼ teaspoon freshly grated
nutmeg

1½ cups 2% low-fat milk

1 16-ounce can pumpkin

½ cup low-fat ricotta cheese

2 tablespoons extra-virgin
olive oil

½ teaspoon balsamic or red
wine vinegar

1 pound black linguine

For a whimsical dinner menu next Halloween, plan your menu in the traditional colors of orange and black. Decorate your table with orange jack-o'-lanterns, black cats, and witches' hats, and serve this black pasta with pumpkin sauce. Black pasta colored with squid ink should be available anywhere you can order fresh pasta.

1. Combine the onion and water in a heavy pot and cook, covered, over low heat until soft. Stir occasionally and add a little more water, if necessary, to prevent scorching. Do not brown. Add the marjoram, salt, pepper, and nutmeg and mix well. Cook uncovered until dry. Add the milk and simmer until reduced by one-third. Remove from the heat and add the pumpkin and ricotta cheese. Mix well and spoon into a blender container. Add 1 tablespoon of the oil and the vinegar and blend until smooth. (Makes about 4 cups sauce.)

2. Cook the pasta al dente, according to package directions (about two minutes for fresh pasta). Drain thoroughly and toss with the remaining tablespoon of oil.

3. To serve place ⅔ cup pasta on each of six plates. Top each serving with ⅔ cup sauce.

Makes six servings

Each serving contains approximately:

Calories: 250	**Cholesterol: 12 mg**
Fat: 8 g	**Sodium: 460 mg**

Opposite top: Spicy Carrot Risotto, page 46.

Opposite left: Thai Peanut Rice, page 51.

Opposite right: Macronade on Rigatoni, page 50.

Macronade on Rigatoni

1 medium onion, finely
  chopped (1½ cups)

1 tablespoon finely chopped
  garlic

½ cup tomato paste

1 cup tomato puree

2 large ripe tomatoes, peeled
  and diced (2 cups)

1 tablespoon sugar

1½ pounds very lean sirloin
  steak, cubed, lightly browned

6 ounces Canadian bacon,
  diced, uncooked

¾ cup dry red wine

½ teaspoon salt

¼ teaspoon freshly ground
  black pepper

Dash of cayenne

1 pound dry rigatoni

During the America's Cup races in San Diego the French team hosted a Soirée Macronade, a typically festive French party where macronade, the hearty pasta dish famous in the region of Sète in the south of France, was served. The party itself was given in honor of the city of Sète, which it was hoped would host the next America's Cup race. After the party many of the guests rooted for the French boat just to be able to go to Sète and have some more of this fabulous dish. When the French team lost their chance to compete in the final race I asked the French chef for his recipe for Macronade so I could host my own "soirée."

1. Combine the onion and garlic in a heavy pot and cook, covered, over very low heat until soft and translucent. Stir occasionally and add a little water or stock, if necessary, to prevent scorching. Add the tomato paste, tomato puree, diced tomatoes, and sugar and mix well. Cook, covered, over low heat, stirring occasionally, for 2 to 3 hours.

2. Add the browned beef, bacon, wine, salt, pepper, and cayenne and mix well. Continue to cook, covered, stirring occasionally, for 2 to 3 more hours.

3. To serve, cook the rigatoni according to the package directions until al dente. Serve the cooked pasta on warm plates and pass the sauce to spoon over the pasta.

Makes 6 cups; six 1-cup servings

Each serving contains approximately:

Calories: 635	Cholesterol: 90 mg
Fat: 19 g	Sodium: 840 mg

Thai Peanut Rice

2 cups cooked brown rice

1 8-ounce can water chestnuts, drained and diced

¼ cup finely chopped green onions

¼ cup chopped cilantro (fresh coriander)

½ cup silken tofu (4 ounces)

1½ teaspoons fresh lime juice

¼ teaspoon salt

1½ teaspoons sugar

6 tablespoons unhomogenized peanut butter

2 teaspoons sodium-reduced soy sauce

1 teaspoon dark sesame oil

½ garlic clove, minced (½ teaspoon)

1 small red pepper, diced, or to taste

2 tablespoons rice vinegar

1 tablespoon water

Green onions, cilantro sprigs, and peppers, for garnish (optional)

This is an unusual vegetarian entree or an exciting side dish with fish, poultry, or meat. Serve hot, room temperature, or cold.

1. Combine the rice, water chestnuts, green onions, and cilantro in a mixing bowl.

2. Combine all remaining ingredients, except the garnish in a blender and blend until smooth.

3. Pour the sauce over the rice mixture and mix well. To serve, put ¾ cup Thai Peanut Rice on each of four plates. If desired, garnish each serving with chopped green onions, cilantro sprigs, and peppers.

Makes 3 cups; four ¾-cup servings

Each serving contains approximately:

Calories: 352   **Cholesterol: None**

Fat: 17 g   **Sodium: 341 mg**

Pasta alla Checca

2 pounds ripe tomatoes (4 cups peeled and diced)

½ teaspoon salt

2 garlic cloves, or to taste, minced

½ cup shredded fresh basil leaves

½ cup chopped fresh parsley

2 tablespoons extra-virgin olive oil

¼ teaspoon freshly ground black pepper, or to taste

¼ teaspoon crushed red pepper flakes, or to taste

12 ounces dry fettuccine

Sprigs of fresh basil, for garnish (optional)

This spicy uncooked pasta sauce served over piping hot fettuccine and topped with a sprinkle of freshly grated Parmigiano-Reggiano is my favorite pasta dish. The secret to success is using really flavorful tomatoes and allowing them to drain long enough to get rid of all the excess water, thereby concentrating the tomato flavor.

1. Plunge the tomatoes into boiling water for 10 seconds to loosen their skins. Peel and dice the tomatoes. Sprinkle with salt and mix well. Place the salted tomatoes in a colander and allow to drain at least 2 hours.

2. Combine the garlic, basil, parsley, olive oil, and black and red pepper. Add the drained tomatoes and mix well.

3. Cook the fettuccine al dente, according to package directions.

4. To serve, place 1½ cups cooked noodles on each of four plates. Top each serving with ¾ cup sauce and garnish with a sprig of fresh basil, if desired.

Makes 3 cups sauce; four ¾-cup servings

Each serving contains approximately:

Calories: 420   **Cholesterol: None**

Fat: 9 g   **Sodium: 325 mg**

Pacific Rim Pizza Quiche, page 59.

Pasta alla Checca.

Macaroni and Cheese

8 ounces dry elbow macaroni
  (2 cups)

1 8-ounce carton nonfat sour
  cream substitute

2 tablespoons corn oil
  margarine

1 medium onion, finely chopped
  (1½ cups)

1 garlic clove, minced

1½ tablespoons unbleached
  all-purpose flour

½ teaspoon salt

½ teaspoon paprika

¼ teaspoon freshly ground
  black pepper

⅛ teaspoon cayenne pepper

2 cups 2% low-fat milk,
  warmed

2 cups (8 ounces) grated 20%
  fat-reduced sharp cheddar
  cheese

¾ cup fresh seeded rye bread
  crumbs (approximately 1
  slice)

This is a variation on my grandmother's recipe for macaroni and cheese. Hers was much higher in fat, but mine is just as creamy. The taste of the caraway seeds in the rye bread crumbs adds a unique dimension to this old-fashioned favorite.

1. Preheat the oven to 350°F. Cook the macaroni according to the package directions. Drain thoroughly, mix with the sour cream substitute, and set aside.

2. Melt the margarine in a heavy saucepan over low heat. Add the onion and garlic and cook, stirring occasionally, until very soft and translucent, about 10 minutes. Stir in the flour, salt, paprika, black pepper, and cayenne pepper and mix well. Cook, stirring constantly, for 3 minutes.

3. Add the milk, a little at a time, and continue cooking, stirring constantly, until smooth and slightly thickened. Remove from the heat and add the cheese, stirring until the cheese is melted.

4. Spray a 2-quart casserole or baking dish with nonstick vegetable coating. Add the macaroni mixture to the casserole. Pour the cheese sauce over the macaroni and mix thoroughly. Sprinkle the bread crumbs over the top and spray them with the nonstick vegetable coating. Bake in the preheated oven until bubbly and a golden brown on top, about 25 to 30 minutes.

Makes 8 cups; eight 1-cup servings

Each serving contains approximately:

Calories: 325   **Cholesterol: 29 mg**

Fat: 12 g   **Sodium: 404 mg**

Pad Thai

(Stir-fried Noodles, Thai Style)

1 pound small-size Thai rice noodles, fresh or dried

1 cup mung bean sprouts

½ cup cold water

2 tablespoons peanut or canola oil

2 tablespoons dried red chilies, or to taste, soaked in water

2 tablespoons minced shallots

1 tablespoon minced garlic

1 tablespoon sugar

3 tablespoons fish sauce

¼ cup fresh lime juice

½ pound shrimp, shelled and deveined (1 cup)

3 egg whites

3 tablespoons pulverized dried shrimp

3 tablespoons finely chopped peanuts

Cilantro (fresh coriander) leaves, for garnish

Green onions, for accompaniment (optional)

Fresh bean sprouts, for accompaniment (optional)

Stir-fried noodles are popular throughout Thailand, particularly in rural areas. This recipe is one I learned to make at The Thai Cooking School in Bangkok and it is my favorite version of this dish. Many of the ingredients are available in the Asian section of the supermarket. However, it may be necessary to go to an Asian market for the small-size rice noodles, dried red chilies, fish sauce, and dried shrimp.

1. If the noodles are dried, soak them in cold water for 15 minutes. Drain thoroughly and set aside.

2. Place the bean sprouts in the water and set aside.

3. In a wok or large frying pan, heat the oil. Add the chilies, shallots, and garlic and stir-fry over medium-high heat until they start to brown. Add the sugar, fish sauce, and lime juice and mix well. Add the shrimp and cook, stirring constantly, until they turn from translucent to opaque. Add the egg whites and stir until they start to set. Add the drained noodles and drain and add the bean sprouts. Toss until well mixed, thoroughly coated, and warm, about 3 minutes.

4. Before serving, top with dried shrimp, peanuts, and cilantro leaves and accompany, if desired, with cilantro leaves and bean sprouts.

Makes 8 cups; six 1½-cup servings

Each serving contains approximately:

Calories: 445

Fat: 8 g

Cholesterol: 79 mg

Sodium: 635 mg

*Top: Pad Thai (Stir-fried
Noodles, Thai Style), page 55.*

*Opposite: Macaroni and Cheese,
page 54.*

Right: Pastitsio, page 58.

Pastitsio

meat mixture:

1 large onion, chopped (2 cups)

1 pound lean ground lamb

1 16-ounce can whole tomatoes, drained and mashed

1 8-ounce can tomato sauce

1/2 teaspoon salt

1/2 teaspoon oregano, crushed with a mortar and pestle

1/4 teaspoon ground cinnamon

1/8 teaspoon freshly ground black pepper

1 slice whole wheat bread, toasted and crumbled (1/2 cup)

white sauce:

3 tablespoons corn oil margarine

1/3 cup whole wheat flour

2 1/2 cups nonfat (skim) milk, simmering

1/2 teaspoon salt

1/4 teaspoon ground cinnamon

1/8 teaspoon white pepper

3 egg whites, lightly beaten

1/2 cup low-fat ricotta cheese

1 16-ounce package tube pasta, cooked according to package directions and well drained

1 cup (4 ounces) grated Romano cheese

This is a wonderful dish you can easily make ahead for parties. I like it hot or at room temperature.

1. To make the meat mixture, in a large covered saucepan over low heat, cook the onion until soft, about 10 minutes. Stir occasionally and add a little water, if necessary, to prevent scorching. Add the lamb and cook until done, about 5 minutes, stirring frequently to keep crumbly. Add the tomatoes, tomato sauce, and seasonings, mix well, cover, and simmer 40 minutes, stirring occasionally. Add the bread crumbs and mix well.

2. Meanwhile, make the white sauce. Melt the margarine in a skillet over medium heat. Add the flour and cook 3 minutes, stirring constantly. Add the milk, stirring constantly until smooth. Add the salt, cinnamon, and white pepper and cook, stirring frequently, until thickened, about 15 minutes. Remove from the heat and slowly add the egg whites, stirring constantly. Combine 1 cup of the white sauce with the ricotta cheese. Mix well and set aside.

3. Preheat the oven to 350°F. Spray a 3-quart baking dish with nonstick vegetable coating. Spread half the cooked pasta in the dish and top with the white sauce without the added ricotta cheese. Spread the meat mixture evenly over the top and then sprinkle half the grated Romano cheese over the meat mixture. Cover with the remaining pasta and bake for 30 minutes.

4. Remove from the oven and increase the oven temperature to 400°F. Spread the reserved white sauce with the ricotta cheese over the top and sprinkle evenly with the remaining Romano cheese. Bake another 20 to 30 minutes, or until slightly browned. Cool 10 minutes before serving.

Makes eight 1 1/2-cup servings

Each serving contains approximately:

Calories: 483   **Cholesterol: 61 mg**

Fat: 13 g   **Sodium: 760 mg**

Pacific Rim
Pizza Quiche

¾ cup finely chopped onion

½ cup chopped roasted red
 pepper (see page 73)

¼ cup chopped fresh parsley

1 garlic clove, minced or
 pressed

1½ cups small broccoli florets,
 blanched

½ cup (2 ounces) freshly
 grated Parmesan cheese

2 cups (1 pound) silken soft
 tofu

4 egg whites

1 tablespoon fresh lemon juice

1 teaspoon dried basil,
 crushed with a mortar and
 pestle

½ teaspoon dried oregano,
 crushed with a mortar and
 pestle

½ teaspoon dried tarragon,
 crushed with a mortar and
 pestle

½ teaspoon salt

¼ teaspoon freshly ground
 black pepper

⅛ teaspoon freshly grated
 nutmeg

2 teaspoons extra-virgin olive
 oil

This dish exemplifies the growing trend of combining flavors and cooking techniques of different cultures and regions. Some people call it "fusion food" and others refer to it as "new alliance cuisine." Whatever name you give to it, this Pacific Rim Pizza Quiche has it all. It's an Italian pizza-flavored French quiche made with tofu! (To enhance its mixed heritage, I cooked the quiche in a French quiche dish and served it on an Adams English ironstone pattern called Chinese Bird. William Adams first introduced a version of this pattern in 1780, and it was one of the earliest patterns in the Chinese style to be produced in English pottery.)

This quiche is excellent served as a brunch, luncheon, or light supper entree. It can also be made in a square pan and cut into small squares to pass as hors d'oeuvre or served as a side dish.

1. Preheat the oven to 425°F. In a nonstick skillet, combine the onion, red pepper, parsley, and garlic. Cook, covered, over low heat until the onion is soft, about 8 to 10 minutes. Stir occasionally and add a little water, if necessary, to prevent scorching.

2. Spoon the cooked onion mixture into a 9-inch quiche dish which has been sprayed with nonstick vegetable coating. Spread the mixture evenly over the bottom of the dish. Top with the broccoli florets and sprinkle the cheese evenly over the top.

3. Combine all the remaining ingredients in a blender or food processor and process on medium-high speed until smooth. Pour the mixture over the cheese and bake for 15 minutes. Reduce the oven temperature to 325°F. and continue to bake for 30 more minutes, or until a knife inserted in the center comes out clean. Allow to stand for 10 minutes before cutting.

Makes 8 servings

Each serving contains approximately:

Calories: 145	**Cholesterol: 4 mg**
Fat: 8 g	**Sodium: 270 mg**

Crab Cakes on Roasted Red Pepper Coulis, page 72.

Thai Baked Squid

Finnish-style Salmon Tartar and Rye Crepes

Horseradish "Cream" Sauce

Som Goong Thai Thai
(Thai Country-style Seafood Curry)

Monkfish Pepper Steaks with Browned Onions

Steamed Monkfish with Seaweed and Vegetables

Browned Onions

Herbed Olive Oil Sauce

Red Wine Sauce

Crisp Salmon with Couscous and Currants

Pla Nueng Prig Manow
(Steamed Fish with Chilies and Lime)

Crab Cakes on Roasted Red Pepper Coulis

Roasted Red Pepper Coulis

Seafood Paella

Sautéed Fish Fillet with Ginger Sauce

Thai Baked Squid

1 large squid (1½ pounds)

½ cup celery leaves

1 stalk lemon grass, crushed

1 bunch cilantro (fresh coriander)

3 tablespoons sliced galanga (Thai ginger), or peeled, sliced fresh ginger

6 garlic cloves

½ cup fresh lime juice

½ cup water

Cooked rice (optional)

Large squid are usually only available in Asian fish markets, as are lemon grass and galanga. You can either serve this as I have, stuffed with rice and surrounded by Thai Country-style Seafood Curry (page 65), or you can serve it by itself with rice and any vegetable of your choice as side dishes.

1. Preheat the oven to 325°F. Carefully pull the mantle or body and the tentacles of the squid apart under cold running water. The head, eye, and ink sac will pull away with the tentacles. Remove the intestines from the mantle, turn it inside out, and wash it thoroughly with cold running water. Pull out the transparent quill and discard. Peel away as much of the skin from the mantle as possible and discard the skin. Rinse again with cold water.

2. Remove the ink sac and eyes from the head and discard. Lay open the tentacles to expose the beak and pull it away and discard. Wash the head and tentacles thoroughly with cold running water.

3. Combine the celery leaves, lemon grass, cilantro, galanga, and garlic and stuff the mantle of the squid with the mixture. Place the stuffed mantle in a flat, noncorrosive baking dish and place the head back in its original position.

4. Mix the lime juice and water and pour over the squid. Cover tightly with a lid or aluminum foil and bake in the preheated oven for 15 to 20 minutes, or until the squid is tender. Remove and discard the stuffing mixture and restuff the squid with cooked rice, if desired. When serving, cut the tentacles free from the head and eyes and discard the head and eyes. Slice the mantle and tentacles into small pieces and serve with rice or your favorite pasta.

Makes six 2-ounce servings

Each serving contains approximately:

Calories: 55   **Cholesterol: 132 mg**

Fat: 1 g   **Sodium: 25 mg**

Finnish-style Salmon Tartar and Rye Crepes

crepes:

⅓ cup whole wheat flour

¼ cup rye flour

¼ teaspoon salt

¼ teaspoon caraway seeds

1 cup nonfat (skim) milk

1 large egg

1 large egg white

1 tablespoon canola or corn oil, plus additional oil for coating the pan

filling:

½ pound salmon fillet, finely chopped

6 ounces sea bass fillet, finely chopped

1 medium shallot, finely chopped

1 tablespoon olive oil

1 tablespoon fresh lemon juice

¼ teaspoon salt

⅛ teaspoon white pepper

1 cup Horseradish "Cream" Sauce (page 64)

1 tablespoon pink peppercorns, for garnish (optional)

1 tablespoon salmon eggs, for garnish (optional)

Fresh dill, for garnish (optional)

When I took the certificate course in fish at the Ritz Cooking School in Paris, this Salmon Tartar was the very first recipe we were taught how to make. We served it with plain crepes and whipped cream seasoned with horseradish. I think that the rye crepes add even more of a Finnish touch to this dish and my Horseradish "Cream" Sauce is fat-free!

1. To make the crepes, combine the flours, salt, and caraway seeds in a bowl and mix well. In another bowl combine the milk, egg, egg white, and oil and whisk until well blended. Pour the liquid ingredients into the dry ingredients and mix well. Allow to stand for 30 minutes before making crepes.

2. To cook the crepes, heat a small skillet or crepe pan. After the pan is hot, wipe the inside with oil. Spoon 2 tablespoons of crepe batter into the pan and tilt from side to side to spread evenly. When the edges start to curl, turn the crepe with a spatula and brown the other side. Place the crepes in a covered container as you make them to keep them pliable.

3. To make the filling, combine the chopped fish, shallot, and olive oil and mix well. Add the lemon juice, salt, and pepper and again mix well. Refrigerate, tightly covered, until ready to serve.

4. To serve, spoon ¼ cup filling onto half of each crepe. Fold the crepe over, pressing lightly to distribute the filling. Serve with dollops of Horseradish "Cream" Sauce. Garnish with a sprinkle of pink peppercorns, salmon eggs, and fresh dill, if desired.

Note: For a prettier presentation cut each crepe into a circle using a pastry cutter, or cut around the edge of a small bowl.

Makes 16 crepes; eight 2-crepe servings

Each serving contains approximately:

Calories: 150   **Cholesterol: 54 mg**

Fat: 6g   **Sodium: 240 mg**

Horseradish "Cream" Sauce

1 1/2 teaspoons (1/2 package) unflavored gelatin

1 tablespoon cool water

2 tablespoons boiling water

1 cup nonfat sour cream substitute

3 tablespoons prepared horseradish

1. Combine the gelatin and cool water and allow the gelatin to soften. Add the boiling water and stir until the gelatin is completely dissolved.

2. Combine the gelatin mixture and all the other ingredients in a food processor and blend until satin-smooth. Refrigerate, tightly covered, until ready to serve.

Makes 1 1/4 cups; ten 2-tablespoon servings

Each serving contains approximately:

Calories: 16   **Cholesterol: None**

Fat: Negligible   **Sodium: 25 mg**

Top: Monkfish Pepper Steaks with Browned Onions, page 66.

Bottom: Finnish-style Salmon Tartar and Rye Crepes, page 63, with Horseradish "Cream" Sauce.

Som Goong Thai Thai

(Thai Country-style Seafood Curry)

1 tablespoon chili paste

5 garlic cloves, minced

7 shallots, minced

1 tablespoon sliced lemon grass

1 teaspoon finely chopped kafir
  lime leaves

3 tablespoons minced galanga
  (Thai ginger), or peeled,
  minced fresh ginger

1 teaspoon shrimp paste

½ cup cooked shrimp

2 cups fish stock or water

⅓ cup tamarind water or lime
  juice

¼ cup fish sauce

2 teaspoons palm sugar, or
  light brown sugar

3 cups blanched mixed vegetables (cauliflower, green
  beans, squash, eggplant, baby
  corn, spinach, etc.)

½ pound raw shrimp, shelled
  and deveined (1 cup)

Cooked rice or oriental noodles
  (optional)

This is another dish I learned to make at The Thai Cooking School in Bangkok. It is an excellent example of the balance of sweet, salty, and spicy found in Thai cooking. This is typically a very spicy dish but if you want to cut back on the heat from the chilies, use less chili paste. This dish will require a trip to a Thai market for the chili paste, lemon grass, kafir lime leaves, galanga, shrimp paste, and fish sauce.

1. Combine the chili paste, garlic, shallots, lemon grass, lime leaves, galanga, and shrimp paste in a mortar and pound with a pestle until smooth (or place in a food processor and blend until smooth). Add the cooked shrimp and again pound or blend until smooth.

2. Bring stock or water to a rapid boil. Add the blended mixture and stir constantly until slightly thickened. Add the tamarind water or lime juice, fish sauce, and sugar and mix well while mixture continues to boil.

3. Add the vegetables and shrimp and continue to cook, stirring constantly, until the shrimp turn from translucent to opaque, 1 to 2 minutes. Immediately remove from heat.

4. Serve with rice or noodles, if desired, or serve with Thai Baked Squid (page 62) stuffed with rice, spooning the curry around the squid. (To serve, slit the squid down the middle of the mantle and spoon the rice onto plates. Top the rice with the curry and a little of the baked squid.)

Makes 6 cups; six 1-cup servings

Each serving contains approximately:

Calories: 115

Fat: 1 g

Cholesterol: 117 mg

Sodium: 835 mg

Monkfish Pepper Steaks with Browned Onions

1¼ pounds monkfish fillets

Flour (for dusting fish)

3 tablespoons coarsely crushed
  black peppercorns

½ teaspoon salt

2 tablespoons corn oil
  margarine

¼ cup cognac

½ cup defatted veal stock

2 cups Browned Onions
  (page 68)

If you're not able to find monkfish, any firm white fish will work. In lieu of the onions, this dish goes nicely with a vegetable gratin or creamed spinach. Conversely, the onions work well with any fish, poultry, or meat.

1. Trim the monkfish fillets, removing all of the pink-colored nerve fibers. Cut the fillets into four "steaks." Flatten each steak slightly by placing it between two sheets of wax paper or in a Ziploc bag and gently pounding it with the side of a meat cleaver or some other heavy, flat object.

2. Pat the fish completely dry before dipping it in the flour so as not to form a paste. After dredging the fish in flour, shake off as much of it as possible and then dip it in the crushed peppercorns. Lightly salt both sides of the fish.

3. In a large skillet over medium-high heat, melt 1 tablespoon of the margarine. Sauté the monkfish pieces about 3 minutes per side, or until they turn from translucent to opaque. Do not overcook. Pour the cognac into the pan with the fish. When it is hot, ignite it and allow the flame to burn out.

4. Remove the fish from the pan and reduce the liquid in the pan until almost dry. Add the stock and return to a boil. Whisk in the remaining tablespoon of margarine and then strain the sauce.

5. To serve, place ½ cup Browned Onions on a warm plate and top with a fish steak. Spoon a little of the sauce over the top of the fish. (For a fancier presentation you can flake the steak out in a circular pattern.)

Makes 4 servings

Each serving contains approximately:

Calories: 300	Cholesterol: 94 mg
Fat: 11 g	Sodium: 527 mg

Steamed Monkfish with Seaweed and Vegetables

1 2-ounce package dried
  seaweed

1 large carrot, peeled

1 fennel bulb

½ bulb celery root, peeled

1 large zucchini

1 tablespoon extra-virgin olive
  oil

1¼ pounds monkfish fillets

2 tablespoons fresh lemon juice

½ teaspoon salt

White pepper

1 cup Herbed Olive Oil Sauce
  (page 68), warmed

This is my favorite dish from the Ritz Cooking School. It is unusual, delicious, beautiful, and easy to make. If monkfish is not available substitute any firm white fish. Dried seaweed is available in any Asian market.

1. Put the dried seaweed in a large bowl and cover with water. Set aside.

2. Cut all of the other vegetables into matchstick-size pieces about 1½ inches long. Steam the vegetables until just crisp-tender starting with the firmest and ending with the most tender (the order in which they are listed). Add vegetables about every 2 minutes. When they are done, toss them with the olive oil and cover to keep warm.

3. Trim the monkfish fillets, removing all of the pink-colored nerve fibers. Cut the fish into 16 medallions and sprinkle each with lemon juice, salt, and white pepper. Place the reconstituted seaweed in a steamer basket over boiling water. Place the fish medallions on top of the seaweed, cover, and steam for about 5 minutes, or until the fish turns from translucent to opaque. Do not overcook.

4. To serve, place a mound of vegetables in the center of each plate. Arrange 4 fish medallions on top of the vegetables. Spoon ¼ cup of the Herbed Olive Oil Sauce around the edge of each serving. Garnish with a few strands of seaweed.

Makes 4 servings

Each serving contains approximately:

Calories: 365   **Cholesterol: 35 mg**

Fat: 22 g   **Sodium: 919 mg**

Browned Onions

2 teaspoons corn oil margarine

2 large onions, thinly sliced and separated into rings

1. Melt the margarine in a large skillet. Add the onions and cook, covered, over low heat until soft, about 10 minutes.

2. Uncover and cook, stirring frequently, over medium heat until a golden brown, about 10–15 minutes.

Makes about 2 cups; four ¹/₂-cup servings

Each serving contains approximately:

Calories: 72   **Cholesterol: None**

Fat: 2 g   **Sodium: 26 mg**

Herbed Olive Oil Sauce

3 tablespoons fresh lemon juice

¹/₃ cup extra-virgin olive oil

1 whole garlic clove, peeled

1 medium tomato, peeled, seeded, and finely diced

¹/₂ teaspoon salt

¹/₄ teaspoon freshly ground black pepper

¹/₃ cup water

1 tablespoon finely chopped fresh basil

1 tablespoon finely chopped fresh parsley

1 tablespoon finely chopped fresh chives

1. Combine the lemon juice and olive oil in a saucepan and mix well. Add the garlic, tomato, salt, and pepper. Cook over medium heat just until warm. Remove and discard the garlic clove, add the water, and mix well. Set aside until needed.

2. Just before serving, reheat the sauce until warm and stir in the basil, parsley, and chives.

Makes 1 cup; four ¹/₄-cup servings

Each serving contains approximately:

Calories: 169   **Cholesterol: None**

Fat: 18 g   **Sodium: 298 mg**

Steamed Monkfish with Seaweed and Vegetables, page 67.

Red Wine Sauce

½ tablespoon extra-virgin olive oil

⅔ cup (4 ounces) finely chopped shallots

¼ cup red wine vinegar

½ cup dry red wine

1⅔ cups defatted fish or chicken stock

¼ teaspoon salt (omit if using salted stock)

¼ teaspoon freshly ground black pepper

⅛ teaspoon fresh or dried rosemary

¼ teaspoon fresh lemon juice

1. Heat the oil in a skillet or saucepan. Add the shallots and cook over medium heat until soft and lightly browned, stirring frequently. Add the vinegar and wine and cook until almost dry. Add the stock, salt, pepper, and rosemary and continue to cook until reduced by half.

2. Spoon the sauce into a blender container and add the lemon juice. Blend until smooth and then pass through a strainer.

Makes ¾ cup sauce; four 3-tablespoon servings

Each serving contains approximately:

Calories: 56 **Cholesterol: None**

Fat: 2 g **Sodium: 184 mg**

Top: Sautéed Fish Fillet with Ginger Sauce, page 75.

Bottom: Crisp Salmon with Couscous and Currants, page 70.

Crisp Salmon with Couscous and Currants

⅓ cup currants

1 ½ cups couscous, or 1
  10-ounce box

2 cups water

¾ teaspoon salt

4 teaspoons corn oil margarine

1 pound salmon fillets, skin
  left on

¼ teaspoon freshly ground
  black pepper

¾ cup Red Wine Sauce
  (page 69)

Fresh rosemary, for garnish
  (optional)

I like both the flavor and the texture combinations of this dish. The sweetness of the currants in the couscous is a nice balance for the slight tartness of the Red Wine Sauce, and the tender couscous is perfect with the crisp fish.

1. Soak the currants in warm water to soften them slightly.

2. Put the couscous in a large bowl. Bring the water and ½ teaspoon of the salt to a boil in a saucepan. Pour the boiling salted water over the couscous and allow to rest until all of the water is absorbed.

3. Drain the currants. Add the drained currants and 2 teaspoons of the margarine to the couscous and toss carefully until well mixed. Cover to keep warm.

4. Cut the fish into four 4-ounce portions. Score the skin in a criss-cross pattern with the tip of a sharp knife. With the remaining salt and the pepper, lightly season the fish just before broiling. Place the fish, skin side up, on a baking sheet which has been sprayed with nonstick vegetable coating. Rub ½ teaspoon of the remaining margarine on the top of each piece of fish. Place the fish under a very hot broiler and cook until the skin is crisp and the flesh is just barely cooked through. (It will continue to cook after it is removed from the heat.)

5. To serve, mound ½ cup of the couscous and currants on each plate, or mold it into a circle using a tartlet circle. Top the couscous with a piece of broiled fish, skin side up. Spoon 3 tablespoons of the Red Wine Sauce around the edge of the couscous and garnish with fresh rosemary, if desired.

Makes 4 servings

Each serving contains approximately:

Calories: 540	Cholesterol: 62 mg
Fat: 14 g	Sodium: 724 mg

Pla Nueng Prig Manow

(Steamed Fish with Chilies and Lime)

1 2-pound whole fish (such as red snapper), scaled and gutted

2 tablespoons sliced galanga (Thai ginger), or 2 tablespoons peeled, sliced fresh ginger

1 stalk lemon grass, crushed, or peel from 1 lemon

4 kafir lime leaves

2 sprigs celery leaves

¼ cup finely chopped red chilies

⅔ cup finely chopped garlic

⅓ cup fish sauce

⅔ cup fresh lime juice

Celery leaves, for garnish

Mint leaves, for garnish

Red peppers, for garnish

This is my favorite Thai fish dish. It is delicate in texture and subtle in seasoning. It also makes a lovely buffet table presentation when garnished as suggested. Whole fish are always available in Thai or Asian markets, as are galanga, lemon grass, kafir lime leaves, and red chilies.

1. Remove the bone from the fish by slicing down each side of the backbone and carefully cutting down each side, against the bones, so that all of the bones can be removed in one piece, leaving the fish intact.

2. Stuff the fish with the galanga, lemon grass, kafir lime leaves, and celery leaves. Place the fish in a steamer and steam for about 15 minutes, or until the fish turns from translucent to opaque. Do not overcook or the fish will fall apart and not make a pretty presentation. (You can also place the fish in a flat baking dish, add a little water, and bake, covered, in a 300°F. oven for 15 to 20 minutes.)

3. While the fish is cooking, combine the chilies, garlic, fish sauce, and lime juice and mix well.

4. Place the cooked fish on a serving platter and spoon the garlic mixture over the top. Garnish with celery and mint leaves and red peppers.

Makes 4 servings

Each serving contains approximately:

Calories: 140   **Cholesterol: 40 mg**

Fat: 2 g   **Sodium: 200 mg**

Crab Cakes on Roasted
Red Pepper Coulis

1 teaspoon canola or corn oil

1 teaspoon fresh lemon juice

2 teaspoons Worcestershire
  sauce

Pinch each: celery salt, white
  pepper, ginger, and paprika

Dash of Tabasco sauce

1 egg white, lightly beaten

1 cup soft whole wheat bread
  crumbs (4 slices of bread)

1 ½ cups (6 ounces) flaked
  crabmeat

2 tablespoons minced onion

1 tablespoons minced celery

Roasted Red Pepper Coulis
  (recipe follows)

A few years ago when I was asked to speak at the Washington Press Club for an International Food Media Conference luncheon, they asked me if I would also plan the menu. Since we were in the middle of "crab country" I decided on these crab cakes.

1. Using a food processor fitted with the metal blade, blend the tofu, oil, lemon juice, Worcestershire sauce, seasonings, and Tabasco sauce until satin-smooth. Spoon the mixture into a bowl, add all the other ingredients, and mix well. Cover tightly and refrigerate until well chilled.

2. Divide the chilled mixture into twelve 3-ounce patties. Cook in a nonstick skillet over medium heat until brown on both sides. Serve with Roasted Red Pepper Coulis.

Makes 12 patties; four 3-patty servings

Each serving contains approximately:

Calories: 237	**Cholesterol: 39 mg**
Fat: 12 g	**Sodium: 365 mg**

Seafood Paella, page 74.

Roasted Red Pepper Coulis

¼ cup red bell peppers, roasted, peeled, and seeded
  (see below)
2 tablespoons canola or corn oil
2 tablespoons unbleached all-purpose flour
1¾ cups defatted chicken stock
Salt to taste (omit if using salted stock)
White pepper to taste
Nutmeg to taste

1. Place the peppers in a food processor and puree until smooth.

2. Heat the oil in a skillet and add the flour. Cook over low heat, stirring constantly, for 3 minutes.

Do not brown. Add the chicken stock, season to taste, and allow to simmer for 20 minutes, stirring occasionally.

3. Stir in the red pepper puree and adjust the seasonings, if necessary. Pass through a strainer and serve, or reheat over low heat, but do not allow the sauce to boil.

Makes 1 cup sauce; four ¼-cup servings
Each serving contains approximately:

Calories: 90	**Cholesterol: Negligible**
Fat: 8 g	**Sodium: 34 mg**

Roasted Bell Peppers

1 pound (about 3 medium) red, yellow, or green
  bell peppers

1. Lay the peppers in a broiling pan or baking dish and broil until their skins blister, 2 to 3 minutes. Turn the peppers with tongs and again place under the broiler. Repeat until all sides of the peppers are completely charred.

2. Once charred, place the peppers in a paper bag (or a heavy plastic freezer bag). Close the bag and set aside for 15 to 20 minutes so the charred skins will steam loose from the flesh.

3. Holding each pepper over a bowl, slit down one side, open it up, and remove and discard the seeds, ribs, and stem. Cut the peppers into 2-to 3-inch pieces, and peel off the loosened skin with a paring knife. The bowl will collect the juices which can then be used to store the peeled peppers if you wish.

Makes about 1 cup; two ½-cup servings
Each serving contains approximately:

Calories: 28	**Cholesterol: None**
Fat: Negligible	**Sodium: 3mg**

Seafood Paella

2 tablespoons extra-virgin
  olive oil

4 garlic cloves, minced
  (4 teaspoons)

2 medium onions, chopped
  (3 cups)

2 small bell peppers, seeds and
  membranes removed, cut in
  strips (1½ cups)

2 cups uncooked rice

½ cup finely chopped fresh
  parsley

2 cups clam juice

2 cups dry white wine

1 8-ounce can tomato sauce
  (1 cup)

1 teaspoon salt

¼ cup fresh lemon juice

½ teaspoon saffron

1 pound bay scallops

1 cup frozen peas, thawed

2 4-ounce jars sliced pimento,
  undrained

8 clams, scrubbed and cleaned
  (see Note)

8 large shrimp, shelled and
  deveined, tails left on

1. Preheat the oven to 350°F. Heat the oil in a large ovenproof skillet or paella pan. Add the garlic, onions, and bell peppers and sauté over medium heat for 5 minutes. Add the rice and parsley and stir until the rice is well coated with oil.

2. Add the clam juice, wine, tomato sauce, salt, lemon juice, and saffron. Mix well and bring to a boil. Cover and place in the preheated oven and bake for 1 hour and 15 minutes, or until all the liquid is absorbed.

3. Remove from the oven and stir in the raw scallops, peas, and pimento. Turn the oven off and return the paella to the oven to keep it warm while cooking the shrimp and clams. Do not leave the paella in the oven for more than 5 minutes.

4. Steam the clams and shrimp until the clams open and the shrimp turn opaque, about 2 to 3 minutes. Do not overcook. Discard any unopened clams. Arrange the shrimp and clams on top of the paella.

5. To serve, spoon 1¼ cups of the rice mixture on each of eight individual plates and top each serving with a shrimp and a clam; or place the paella pan in the center of the table and let guests help themselves.

Makes 8 servings

Each serving contains approximately:

Calories: 375   **Cholesterol: 75 mg**

Fat: 6 g   **Sodium: 930 mg**

Note: Place the clams in a large bowl and cover with cold water and 2 tablespoons salt. Sprinkle 2 tablespoons cornmeal over the top and refrigerate for 3 to 12 hours. Drain and rinse well. (This procedure will whiten the shells, remove the sand, and cause the clams to eject the black material in their stomachs.)

Sautéed Fish Fillet
with Ginger Sauce

1 tablespoon corn oil
  margarine

4 shallots (6 ounces), julienne
  cut (1 cup)

1 cup champagne

1 cup fish stock or defatted
  chicken stock

1 ounce fresh ginger root, peeled
  and julienne cut
  (¼ cup)

1 tablespoon extra-virgin olive
  oil

4 fillets (1½ pounds) John
  Dory (St. Peter's fish) or
  other firm white fish

8 green onions, cut diagonally
  into 1-inch pieces

4 cherry tomatoes, baked at
  350°F. for 10 minutes

I first had this dish at Pierrot, the French restaurant on top of the Mandarin Oriental Hotel in Hong Kong. I told their executive chef, Jürg Münch, that I thought it was the most fabulous fish I'd ever had and that I would love to have his recipe. He was kind enough to send it to me and now I'm including it in this book especially for anyone who shares my passion for fresh ginger.

1. Melt the margarine in a heavy skillet. Add the shallots and cook over medium heat until soft and translucent. Add the champagne and reduce by two-thirds. Add the stock and again reduce by two-thirds. Add the ginger, reduce the heat to low, and simmer the ginger sauce for 6 minutes.

2. In another skillet, heat the oil. Cook the fish over medium-high heat until it turns from translucent to opaque, about 2 to 3 minutes per side. Remove the fish and place it on a hot plate to keep it warm. In the same pan, stir-fry the white part of the green onions until they can be pierced with a fork, about 2 minutes. Add the green onion tops and cook just until bright green.

3. To serve, top each fillet with ¼ cup ginger sauce and a sprinkle of green onions. Garnish with baked cherry tomatoes.

Makes 4 servings

Each serving contains approximately:

Calories: 265   **Cholesterol: 94 mg**

Fat: 9 g   **Sodium: 175 mg**

Soft Chicken Tacos, page 78.

Soft Chicken Tacos

Chicken Calvados on Cinnamon Pasta

Mango or Papaya Salsa

Light Aïoli

Chicken Stew Provençal

Turkey Pâté

Creamy Herbed Mustard Dip

Herbed Paillard of Chicken Breast

Turkey Enchiladas

Chicken Maquechoux

Chicken Satay with Spicy Peanut Sauce

Spicy Peanut Sauce

White Chicken Chili

Chicken Mole

poultry

Soft Chicken Tacos

1 tablespoon whole cumin seed

2 medium onions, coarsely chopped (3 cups)

3 garlic cloves, finely minced (1 tablespoon)

1 pound boneless, skinless chicken breast, cubed

2 large fresh tomatoes, coarsely chopped (1½ cups)

2 roasted jalapeño peppers, seeded, deveined, and finely chopped (2 tablespoons)

1 7-ounce can chopped green chilies

1 teaspoon salt

18 corn or whole wheat flour tortillas, warmed

Mango or Papaya Salsa (page 80)

These tasty tacos are good served with just a regular tomato salsa, but I think they are even better and certainly more unusual with a tropical fruit salsa. Try serving Mango or Papaya Salsa, or both, for your next fiesta.

1. Toast the cumin seeds in a heavy skillet over medium heat until golden brown. Stir occasionally and watch carefully because they burn easily. Set aside.

2. Combine the onions and garlic in a large covered skillet or saucepan over low heat. Cook, stirring occasionally, until tender, about 15 to 20 minutes. Add a little water or stock if necessary to prevent scorching. Add the remaining ingredients (except for the tortillas and salsa) and the cumin seed and cook until hot and bubbly and the chicken is no longer pink, about 20 minutes. This is best if made a day ahead.

3. To serve, spoon ⅓ cup taco filling onto each soft, warm tortilla and fold in half. Garnish with ⅓ cup of salsa, as desired.

Makes 6 cups filling; eighteen tacos

Each taco (without salsa) contains approximately:

Calories: 120   **Cholesterol: 19 mg**

Fat: 2 g   **Sodium: 347 mg**

Chicken Calvados on Cinnamon Pasta

½ cup Calvados

¼ cup seedless raisins

½ medium onion, finely chopped (¾ cup)

1 large green apple, peeled and chopped (1 cup)

1 cup defatted chicken stock

½ cup canned evaporated skim milk

½ teaspoon apple cider vinegar

¼ teaspoon dried thyme, crushed with a mortar and pestle

⅛ teaspoon salt (omit if using salted stock)

Dash of freshly ground black pepper

1 cup cooked linguine or fettuccine, drained

1 teaspoon canola or corn oil

½ teaspoon ground cinnamon, plus additional for sprinkling

1 whole chicken breast, boned, skinned, halved, and sautéed

8 baby carrots, steamed

1½ cups haricots verts (tiny green beans), steamed

2 sprigs fresh thyme, for garnish (optional)

I love the combination of cinnamon, apples, and Calvados, but when I first conceived this recipe, I worried that the chicken and the pasta would throw off the flavor range. Happily they didn't, and the result is an unusually tasty dish. If you wish you can substitute cooked rice for the pasta called for in this recipe. Just mix the rice with the oil and cinnamon. However, I think pasta makes a prettier presentation.

1. Several hours ahead of time, pour the Calvados over the raisins to marinate them.

2. Remove the raisins from the Calvados and set aside. Pour the Calvados into a pan and add the onion and apple. Bring to a boil, reduce the heat, and simmer 10 minutes or until dry. Add the stock and milk. Simmer, uncovered, for 30 minutes, stirring occasionally. The sauce will break down and look like curdled milk at this point. Pour the sauce into a blender or food processor and add the vinegar, thyme, salt, and pepper. Blend until smooth. Push through a strainer with the back of a spoon.

3. To serve, toss the drained pasta with the oil and cinnamon. Place a swirled ½-cup mound of pasta on each of two warm plates. Arrange the chicken on top of the pasta and top each serving with ½ cup sauce and 2 tablespoons raisins. Sprinkle with ground cinnamon. Surround the chicken with the carrots and green beans (and the thyme sprigs, if you wish) or arrange as desired.

Makes 2 servings

Each serving contains approximately:

Calories: 516

Fat: 8 g

Cholesterol: 75 mg

Sodium: 352 mg

Chicken Calvados on Cinnamon Pasta, page 79.

Mango or Papaya Salsa

2 pounds ripe mangoes or papayas, peeled,
pitted, and finely diced (3 cups)
1 shallot, minced (1 tablespoon)
1 jalapeño pepper, seeded, deveined, and finely
chopped (1 tablespoon)
1 garlic clove, minced (1 teaspoon)
2 tablespoons tightly packed minced cilantro
(fresh coriander)
1 tablespoon rice vinegar
1 teaspoon fresh lime juice

To make the salsa, combine the mango or papaya and all remaining ingredients. Mix well, cover, and refrigerate for several hours before serving.

Makes 3 cups salsa; nine 1/3-cup servings
Each serving contains approximately:
Papaya:

Calories: 42	**Cholesterol: None**
Fat: Negligible	**Sodium: 17 mg**

Mango:

Calories: 68	**Cholesterol: None**
Fat: Negligible	**Sodium: 16 mg**

Light Aïoli

1 cup (8 ounces) silken firm tofu

2 tablespoons fresh lemon juice

2 tablespoons extra-virgin olive oil

1 tablespoon minced garlic (3 large cloves)

½ teaspoon salt

⅛ teaspoon freshly ground black pepper

Combine all the ingredients in a blender container and blend until satin-smooth.

Makes 1 cup; eight 2-tablespoon servings

Each serving contains approximately:

Calories: 54   **Cholesterol: None**

Fat: 5 g   **Sodium: 150 mg**

Chicken Stew Provençal with Light Aïoli, page 82.

Chicken Stew Provençal with Light Aïoli

3 medium onions, coarsely
   chopped (4½ cups)

3 fennel bulbs, including
   "fern," coarsely chopped
   (9 cups)

4 large tomatoes, peeled and
   coarsely chopped (4 cups)

6 garlic cloves, pressed or
   minced

3 bay leaves

1½ tablespoons dried thyme,
   crushed with mortar and
   pestle

1 teaspoon salt (omit if using
   salted stock)

¾ teaspoon freshly ground
   black pepper

¼ teaspoon cayenne pepper

½ cup Pernod

8 whole chicken legs with thighs
   attached (3 pounds), skinned
   and thigh bones removed

16 small new potatoes
   (2 pounds), or 4 medium
   potatoes, scrubbed and cubed
   (4 cups)

2 cups defatted chicken stock

Light Aïoli (page 81)

When I taught a cooking class at the D'Gustibus Cooking School at Macy's in New York last fall, this is the entree I selected to demonstrate because it is my own favorite recipe for spur-of-the-moment dinner parties. I was delighted that it was also an enormous hit with the students in the class. If you think the ingredients in the Light Aïoli sound a bit bizarre, don't be put off by them. Try it—you'll like it. Not only does it have the taste and texture of "real" aïoli made with egg yolks, it contains no cholesterol!

1. In a large pot or soup kettle, combine the onions, fennel, tomatoes, garlic, bay leaves, thyme, salt, and pepper and mix well. Add ¼ cup of the Pernod, cover, and slowly bring to a boil. Reduce the heat and simmer for 30 minutes.

2. Add the chicken legs to the pot, burying them in the mixture so that they will absorb the flavor as they cook. Continue to simmer, covered, for 30 more minutes.

3. While the stew is cooking, combine the potatoes and chicken stock in another pan and cook until the potatoes can be easily pierced with a fork. Add the potatoes and all of the stock in the pan to the stew. Add the remaining ¼ cup Pernod and simmer, covered, for 30 more minutes.

4. To serve, spoon approximately 2 cups stew and a chicken leg into each of eight large bowls. Top with a dollop of Light Aïoli, if desired.

Makes 8 servings

Each serving contains approximately:

Calories: 340	**Cholesterol: 93 mg**
Fat: 10 g	**Sodium: 595 mg**

Turkey Pâté

1 tablespoon canola or corn
  oil

½ medium onion, finely
  chopped (¾ cup)

2 garlic cloves, finely chopped

¾ pound fresh mushrooms,
  finely chopped

½ cup dry sherry

1 egg plus 2 egg whites

1 teaspoon salt

¾ teaspoon dried thyme,
  crushed with a mortar and
  pestle

¼ teaspoon ground allspice

¼ teaspoon ground mace

⅛ teaspoon freshly ground
  black pepper

1 teaspoon Tabasco sauce

2 pounds ground turkey

½ cup finely chopped fresh
  parsley

1 cup quick-cooking oatmeal

Creamy Herbed Mustard Dip
  (page 84)

*This pâté is fabulous for country picnics and everyday brown bag
lunches alike. When packing it for travel, wrap each slice separately or
put a couple in tightly sealed individual plastic sandwich bags. Throw
in a crusty baguette, a container of Creamy Herbed Mustard Dip, and
some fresh fruit—and off you go with a portable feast!*

1. Preheat the oven to 350°F. Heat the oil in a deep saucepan over
low heat. Add the onion, garlic, and mushrooms and mix well.
Cook, covered, until the onion is soft and translucent, about 10
minutes. Remove the lid, increase the heat to medium-high, and
cook, stirring frequently, until all of the liquid has cooked away.
Add the sherry and cook for 5 more minutes. Set aside to cool.

2. Combine the egg, egg whites, salt, thyme, allspice, mace,
pepper, and Tabasco sauce in a large mixing bowl and mix well.
Add the ground turkey, parsley, and oatmeal and mix well. Add
the mushroom mixture and again mix well.

3. Spoon the mixture into a standard-size loaf pan that has been
sprayed with nonstick vegetable coating. Press down firmly to
shape into a loaf. Bake for 45 minutes, remove from the oven, and
pour off the juices. Return to the oven and continue to bake for
another 30 minutes. Remove from the oven and place on a rack
to cool. When cool, invert the pâté onto a large piece of aluminum
foil and wrap tightly. Refrigerate overnight before serving.

4. To serve, cut into sixteen ½-inch slices. For picnics, wrap each
slice separately or put them in tightly sealed individual plastic
sandwich bags. Serve with Creamy Herbed Mustard Dip.

Makes 16 servings

Each serving (without spread) contains approximately:

Calories: 155   **Cholesterol: 57 mg**

Fat: 8 g   **Sodium: 213 mg**

Creamy Herbed Mustard Dip

1 cup nonfat sour cream substitute

2 tablespoons Dijon mustard

1 teaspoon canola or corn oil

½ teaspoon dried thyme, crushed with a mortar and pestle

½ teaspoon Pernod

¼ teaspoon ground anise seed

¼ teaspoon salt

⅛ teaspoon freshly ground black pepper

Place all the ingredients in a blender and process on high speed until completely smooth.

Makes 1 cup; sixteen 1-tablespoon servings

Each serving contains approximately:

Calories: 14   **Cholesterol: None**

Fat: Negligible   **Sodium: 73 mg**

Top: Turkey Pàté, page 83.

Bottom: Herbed Paillard of Chicken Breast, opposite.

Herbed Paillard of
Chicken Breast

8 boneless, skinless chicken
  breast halves

Juice of 1 large lemon

½ cup whole wheat flour

1 teaspoon freshly ground black
  pepper

½ teaspoon salt

1 teaspoon dried thyme, crushed
  with a mortar and pestle

1 teaspoon dried sage, crushed
  with a mortar and pestle

¼ teaspoon fresh or dried
  rosemary leaves, crushed with
  a mortar and pestle

4 egg whites, lightly beaten

2 cups whole wheat bread
  crumbs

2 tablespoons chopped fresh
  parsley

2 tablespoons extra-virgin olive
  oil

This is another recipe that I perfected while attending Ann Clark's cooking school, La Bonne Cuisine, in Austin, Texas. It was the first time I had ever used a Ziploc plastic bag instead of wax paper to cover the chicken while pounding it. Now I routinely do it because I agree with Ann that it works better.

1. Place each chicken breast half, in turn, in a small Ziploc bag (this works better than wax paper). Pound each piece to a thickness of ¼ inch with the back of a large spoon or the flat side of a meat tenderizer. Rub each piece with lemon juice.

2. Combine the flour, pepper, salt, thyme, sage, and rosemary on a dinner plate. Place the egg whites on another plate. Combine the bread crumbs and parsley on another plate.

3. Heat about 2 teaspoons of the oil in a large nonstick skillet over medium-high heat. Dredge the chicken breasts in the seasoned flour and shake off the excess. Dip each in the beaten egg whites and, finally, in the bread crumbs.

4. Cook the breaded chicken breasts in the skillet, about 3 minutes per side or until the chicken turns white and is firm to the touch. Add more oil, as needed. Be careful not to overcook the chicken or it will be dry and tough.

Makes 8 servings

Each serving contains approximately:

Calories: 306   **Cholesterol: 74 mg**

Fat: 8 g   **Sodium: 422 mg**

Turkey Enchiladas

1 medium onion, chopped
  (1½ cups)

2 large tomatoes, peeled and
  chopped (2½ cups)

2 teaspoons chopped, seeded,
  and deveined jalapeño
  peppers

1 7-ounce can chopped
  California green chilies,
  drained

1 cup (1 8-ounce can) tomato
  sauce

1 teaspoon dried oregano,
  crushed with a mortar and
  pestle

1 4-ounce package light cream
  cheese (Neufchâtel), softened

2 tablespoons nonfat (skim)
  milk

½ teaspoon ground cumin

½ teaspoon salt

2 cups chopped cooked turkey

8 corn tortillas, warmed so
  they won't crack when rolled

1 cup (4 ounces) grated 20%
  fat-reduced Monterey Jack
  cheese

Chopped green onions, for
  garnish

Cilantro (fresh coriander), for
  garnish (optional)

I prefer making these enchiladas in individual au gratin dishes rather than one large baking dish because the presentation is so much more attractive. I like to serve a tossed green salad with lots of cilantro in it on the side.

1. In a large covered saucepan over very low heat, sweat the onion until soft, about 10 minutes. Stir occasionally and add a little water if necessary to prevent scorching. Add the tomatoes, jalapeño, green chilies, tomato sauce, and oregano and simmer, covered, for 30 minutes.

2. Preheat the oven to 350°F. While the sauce is simmering, combine the cream cheese, milk, cumin, and salt and mix well. Stir in the turkey. Roll ¼ cup filling in each tortilla and place, seam side down, in a 9 x 13-inch baking dish sprayed with nonstick vegetable coating, or place in individual sprayed au gratin dishes.

3. Top each enchilada with ½ cup sauce and cover with aluminum foil. Bake in the preheated oven for 30 minutes. Remove and discard the foil and sprinkle the cheese over the sauce. Return to the oven for another 15 minutes, or until the cheese is melted and the sauce is hot and bubbly.

Makes 8 servings

Each serving contains approximately:

Calories: 230   **Cholesterol: 40 mg**

Fat: 9 g   **Sodium: 850 mg**

Chicken
Maquechoux

6 chicken thighs, skinned and
   all visible fat removed

¼ cup dry white wine

2 medium onions, finely
   chopped (3 cups)

¾ cup (5 ounces) diced green
   bell pepper

1½ pounds ripe plum toma-
   toes, chopped (3 cups)

¾ teaspoon salt

1 teaspoon freshly ground black
   pepper

½ teaspoon dried basil, crushed
   with a mortar and pestle

½ teaspoon dried thyme,
   crushed with a mortar and
   pestle

½ teaspoon dried tarragon,
   crushed with a mortar and
   pestle

2 to 3 ears fresh corn, grated (1
   cup)

3 ears fresh corn kernels
   (1½ cups)

6 sprigs of fresh thyme or
   tarragon, for garnish
   (optional)

"Maquechoux" is a Cajun word meaning a smothered dish made with fresh corn. Grating the corn rather than just cutting it off the cob is an important first step in this recipe. The grating "milks" the juices from the fresh corn cob and adds more flavor to the dish.

1. In a nonstick skillet, cook the chicken thighs over medium-low heat until they are a deep golden brown on both sides, about 10–15 minutes. Add the wine and continue to cook, covered, until all the wine is absorbed, about 10 minutes.

2. While the chicken thighs are browning, combine the onions, bell pepper, tomatoes, salt, pepper, basil, thyme, and tarragon in a large skillet or saucepan. Cook over low heat, covered, for 20 minutes, stirring occasionally. Add all of the corn and stir until well mixed. Add the chicken thighs, burying them in the mixture. Continue to simmer, covered, for 15 minutes more.

3. To serve, place a chicken thigh in a soup or gumbo bowl. Spoon 1 cup sauce over the top. Garnish with sprigs of fresh thyme or tarragon, if desired.

Makes 6 servings

Each serving contains approximately:

Calories: 217

Cholesterol: 54 mg

Fat: 7 g

Sodium: 362 mg

Chicken Satay with Spicy Peanut Sauce

¼ cup sodium-reduced soy
  sauce

¼ cup dry sherry

2 tablespoons rice vinegar

2 tablespoons fresh lemon juice

1 garlic clove, minced

2 teaspoons sugar

¼ teaspoon ground cinnamon

Dash of cayenne pepper, or to
  taste

Dash of freshly ground black
  pepper, or to taste

1 pound boneless, skinless
  chicken breast, cut in 1-inch
  strips

Spicy Peanut Sauce (recipe
  follows)

I first tasted this mouth-watering combination of flavors in Malaysia at a hawker's stand in Kuala Lumpur. From the first bite I was hooked. As soon as I returned home I started making my own healthier version of this Asian treat which is terrific served with Thai Cucumber Salad (page 26).

1. Combine the soy sauce, sherry, vinegar, lemon juice, garlic, sugar, cinnamon, and cayenne and black peppers until well blended. Pour over the chicken and allow to marinate, tightly covered in the refrigerator, for at least 30 to 60 minutes. Meanwhile soak 24 wooden skewers in water.

2. Remove the chicken from the marinade and place each piece on a skewer. Cook over hot coals or under a preheated broiler for about 4 minutes per side, or until the chicken is just done. Do not overcook.

3. Serve on the skewers with Spicy Peanut Sauce for dipping.

Makes about 24 appetizer-size servings

Each serving contains approximately:

Calories: 46   **Cholesterol: 14 mg**

Fat: 2 g   **Sodium: 27 mg**

*Chicken Satay with Spicy
Peanut Sauce.*

Spicy Peanut Sauce

¼ cup chunky-style unhomogenized peanut butter,
  at room temperature

¼ cup plain nonfat yogurt

¼ garlic clove, minced or pressed

1 teaspoon sugar

½ teaspoon sodium-reduced soy sauce

¼ teaspoon dark sesame oil

⅛ teaspoon crushed red pepper flakes, or to taste

1 tablespoon water

Combine all the ingredients in a mixing bowl
and mix well using a wire whisk or a pastry
blender.

Makes ½ cup; twenty-four 1-teaspoon servings

Each serving contains approximately:

Calories: 18   **Cholesterol: Negligible**

Fat: 1 g   **Sodium: 6 mg**

White Chicken Chili, page 90.

Turkey Enchiladas, page 86.

White Chicken Chili

1 pound dried Great Northern beans, soaked overnight (see Note)

2 medium onions, finely chopped (3 cups)

4 garlic cloves, minced (4 teaspoons)

6 cups defatted chicken stock

1 7-ounce can diced green chilies, undrained

2 teaspoons ground cumin

1½ teaspoons dried oregano, crushed with a mortar and pestle

1 teaspoon salt (omit if using salted stock)

1 teaspoon ground coriander

⅛ teaspoon ground cloves

⅛ teaspoon cayenne pepper, or to taste

4 cups diced cooked skinless chicken or turkey breast

1 cup (4 ounces) grated jalapeño Jack cheese

I originally developed this recipe for Neiman Marcus when I was creating an entire Light Cuisine menu for their Newport Beach, California, store. It was a favorite with guests in the restaurant and I'm sure it will be a crowd-pleaser for you too.

1. Drain the beans thoroughly, rinse well, and set aside.

2. Combine the onions and garlic in a heavy 4-quart pot or saucepan and cook, covered, over very low heat, until soft and translucent, about 10 to 15 minutes. Stir occasionally and add a little water or stock, if necessary, to prevent scorching.

3. Add the drained beans and chicken stock and bring to a boil. Reduce the heat to low and cook, covered, for 1 hour. Add all the remaining ingredients except the chicken and cheese and continue to cook, covered, for 1 more hour. Just before serving add the diced chicken or turkey and heat thoroughly.

4. To serve, spoon 1½ cups chili into each of eight warm bowls and top with 2 tablespoons grated cheese.

Makes 12 cups; eight 1½-cup servings
Each serving contains approximately:

Calories: 455	**Cholesterol: 61 mg**
Fat: 8 g	**Sodium: 817 mg**

Variation: *Seafood Chili:* Instead of chicken or turkey, add 2 cups diced cooked fish, shrimp, crab, lobster, clams, scallops, or squid.

Note: For a much faster chili, substitute four 16-ounce cans Great Northern beans, drained (6 cups), for the dried beans. Use only 2 cups stock and omit the salt. Add all the ingredients, except the chicken and cheese, and simmer for 20 to 30 minutes instead of 2 hours.

Chicken Mole

1 medium onion, finely chopped
  (1½ cups)

2 garlic cloves, finely chopped

1 16-ounce can ready-cut
  tomatoes

¼ cup raisins, finely chopped

½ cup chopped cilantro (fresh
  coriander)

⅓ cup chili powder

¼ cup unsweetened cocoa
  powder

½ teaspoon salt (omit if using
  salted stock)

1 tablespoon sugar

1 teaspoon ground cinnamon

½ teaspoon ground cumin

¼ teaspoon ground anise seed

¼ cup unhomogenized smooth
  peanut butter

3 cups defatted chicken stock

8 whole chicken thighs, cooked
  and skinned

When I lived in Mexico City I always served Turkey Mole for Thanksgiving with lots of corn tortillas instead of dressing. Now I use this recipe for Chicken Mole when I'm entertaining because it is much easier to prepare for a smaller group.

1. Cook the onion, covered, over low heat until soft, stirring frequently. Add a little water or stock, if necessary, to prevent scorching. Add all the other ingredients except the chicken stock and chicken thighs. Mix well and cook, uncovered, over medium heat, stirring frequently, for about 10 minutes.

2. Bring the stock to a boil and add it to the mole sauce. Cook over very low heat, stirring occasionally, for 45 minutes.

3. To serve, heat the chicken and pour ½ cup of the sauce over the top of each chicken thigh or add the thighs to the sauce and serve as you would a stew.

Makes 8 servings

Each serving contains approximately:

Calories: 285   **Cholesterol: 77 mg**

Fat: 10 g   **Sodium: 455 mg**

Cassoulet Provençal, page 106.

Beef Fajitas

Pittsfield Stew

Tarragon Dumplings

Red and Yellow Salsa

Malaysian Steamboat

meat

Swedish Meatballs

Finnish Venison Stew

Hoppin' John

Olde English Cottage Pie

Green Eggs and Ham en Croustade

Cassoulet Provençal

Rabbit in Mustard Sauce

Gingered Beef Stir-fry on Sesame Chuka Soba Noodles

Cantonese Sweet-and-Sour Pork

Beef Fajitas

2 pounds flank steak, all
 visible fat removed and cut
 with the grain into
 ½-inch-thick strips

2 medium onions, thinly sliced
 (4 cups)

⅔ cup fresh lime juice

5 garlic cloves, finely chopped

½ teaspoon freshly ground
 black pepper

1½ teaspoons ground cumin

1 teaspoon dried oregano,
 crushed with a mortar and
 pestle

1 large red bell pepper, seeds
 and membranes removed,
 cut into thin strips

1 large green bell pepper, seeds
 and membranes removed,
 cut into thin strips

12 whole wheat flour tortillas,
 wrapped in aluminum foil
 and warmed in a 300°F.
 oven 15 minutes

Red and Yellow Salsa
 (page 97)

Cilantro (fresh coriander)
 leaves, for garnish
 (optional)

This colorful and spicy combination of ingredients is classically served on a sizzling skillet. Guests help themselves, placing the hot mixture in the middle of a tortilla, rolling it up, and eating it with salsa.

1. Place the beef and onions in a 9 x 13-inch glass or nonaluminum baking dish and set aside.

2. Mix together the lime juice, garlic, black pepper, cumin, and oregano. Pour over the beef and onions, cover, and let marinate 2 to 4 hours in the refrigerator, stirring occasionally.

3. Heat a large nonstick skillet over medium-high heat and add the beef and onions, the bell peppers, and enough of the marinade (1 to 2 tablespoons) to keep the mixture from sticking. Stir-fry just until beef is no longer pink. Do not overcook.

4. Place about ½ cup of the mixture in the center of a warm tortilla. Top with salsa and cilantro, if desired. Fold up the bottom of the tortilla, then fold in the sides to enclose. Eat out of hand.

Makes 12 fajitas

Each fajita contains approximately:

Calories: 300	**Cholesterol: 41 mg**
Fat: 13 g	**Sodium: 45 mg**

Pittsfield Stew

1 1/2 pounds top sirloin, all
   visible fat removed, cubed

1 teaspoon red wine vinegar

3/4 teaspoon salt

1/2 teaspoon freshly ground
   black pepper

1/2 teaspoon sugar

1/4 teaspoon dry mustard

1/4 cup dry red wine

1/2 teaspoon dried tarragon,
   crushed with a mortar and
   pestle

1/2 teaspoon dried oregano,
   crushed with a mortar and
   pestle

1 28-ounce can ready-cut
   tomatoes

2 cups diced potatoes

1 cup sliced celery

1 large onion, cubed

Tarragon Dumplings
   (page 96)

I have no idea where the name for this recipe originated. It was sent to me for revision by a man from Louisiana who had first eaten it at a friend's home in Seattle. The only Pittsfield I know about is in Massachusetts, so your guess is as good as mine. Regardless of its origin, this hearty one-dish meal is easy to make, inexpensive, and a sure hit with guests.

1. Brown the meat over medium-high heat in a heavy pot that has been sprayed with nonstick vegetable coating. Stir occasionally to assure even browning.

2. While the meat is browning, combine the vinegar and salt in a small bowl and stir until the salt is dissolved. Stir in the pepper, sugar, mustard, wine, tarragon, and oregano and mix well. Add the mixture to the browned meat and bring to a boil.

3. Add the tomatoes and reduce the heat to low. Cover and simmer for 1 hour. Add the remaining vegetables, cover, and continue cooking 30 more minutes.

4. While the vegetables are simmering, make the dumplings. Drop the dumplings by tablespoonful onto the hot stew. Cover and simmer for about 20 minutes, or until a knife inserted in the dumplings comes out clean. To serve, place a dumpling on each plate and top with stew.

Makes eight 1-cup servings

Each serving contains approximately:

Calories: 375   **Cholesterol: 70 mg**

Fat: 19 g   **Sodium: 794 mg**

Tarragon Dumplings

1 cup unbleached all-purpose flour

2 teaspoons baking powder

¼ teaspoon salt

¾ teaspoon dried tarragon, crushed with a
  mortar and pestle

1 cup (4 ounces) grated 20% fat-reduced sharp
  cheddar cheese

½ cup nonfat (skim) milk

2 tablespoons canola or corn oil

1. Combine the flour, baking powder, salt, tarragon, and grated cheese in a medium-size bowl
and mix well.

2. Combine the milk and oil and add it to the
flour mixture, stirring just until the dry ingredients are moistened. Do not overmix. Drop by
tablespoonful into the hot stew. Cover and cook
about 20 minutes or until a knife inserted in the
center comes out clean.

Makes 8 dumplings

Each dumpling contains approximately:

Calories: 135   **Cholesterol: 12 mg**

Fat: 7 g   **Sodium: 300 mg**

Top: Beef Fajitas, page 94.

*Bottom: Pittsfield Stew, page 95, with
Tarragon Dumplings.*

Red and Yellow Salsa

When working with hot peppers, be sure never to touch your face or eyes. If your skin is sensitive, wearing rubber gloves is recommended.

1 cup (¹/₂ pound) finely diced yellow tomatoes

1 cup (¹/₂ pound) finely diced red tomatoes

1 small onion, finely diced
(1 cup)

¹/₄ cup coarsely chopped cilantro (fresh coriander)

1 small jalapeño pepper, seeded, deveined, and
finely chopped

1 garlic clove, finely chopped (1 teaspoon)

³/₄ teaspoon ground cumin

³/₄ teaspoon dried oregano, crushed with a mortar
and pestle

¹/₈ teaspoon salt

2 tablespoons fresh lime juice

Combine all the ingredients and mix well. Cover and refrigerate for at least 2 hours before serving.

Makes 1¹/₂ cups; twelve 2-tablespoon servings

Each serving contains approximately:

Calories: 7   **Cholesterol: None**

Fat: Negligible   **Sodium: 20 mg**

Malaysian Steamboat, page 98.

Malaysian Steamboat

cooking ingredients:

6 ounces scallops

6 ounces medium-size shrimp,
   peeled and deveined

6 ounces firm white fish, cubed

6 ounces boneless, skinless
   chicken breast, cubed

6 ounces lean beef, all visible
   fat removed, cubed

8 ounces silken firm tofu,
   cubed

6 cups shredded cabbage

6 cups spinach leaves,
   deveined

stock ingredients:

12 cups defatted chicken stock

1 teaspoon salt (omit if using
   salted stock)

8 green onions, cut diagonally
   into 1-inch pieces

One 3-inch piece peeled fresh
   ginger root, thinly sliced

dipping sauces:

Soy sauce

Chinese hot mustard

Fish sauce

Hoisin sauce

The sauces served with this "do-it-yourself" dinner are a good example of the fascinating crosscultural cuisine of Malaysia. Most of its dishes are influenced by the exotic racial mix of the population that is made up of Malays, Chinese, Indians, and a sprinkling of Europeans. The Malaysian Steamboat is both delicious and tremendous fun to serve for a party.

The cooking pots and the little baskets we used are available in most Asian markets. If you don't have a Malaysian Steamboat, a kettle on a hot plate in the middle of your table will do the trick. Or you can cook this yourself in the kitchen and present the finished product to your guests.

1. Place all the cooking ingredients in small bowls around the cooking pot. Replenish the vegetables during the cooking process, as necessary.

2. If using unsalted stock, add the salt to the stock and mix well. Fill the cooking pot with stock until about two-thirds full. Add some green onion and ginger to the stock and bring to a boil.

3. Have each guest pick up pieces of food to be cooked with chopsticks or a fork and cook them in the simmering stock. The vegetables cook in less than 1 minute and the other ingredients will take from 1 to 3 minutes.

4. When cooked, each guest retrieves the food from the stock with a small basket and places it in his or her bowl. This process continues until all the food is cooked, adding more stock, green onion, and ginger, as necessary, to keep the cooking liquid at the appropriate level and prevent the food from scorching. When all the food is cooked, any remaining stock is served as a soup.

Makes 6 servings

Each serving contains approximately:

Calories: 235	**Cholesterol: 93 mg**
Fat: 9 g	**Sodium: 255 mg**

Swedish Meatballs

2 tablespoons corn oil margarine

1 medium onion, finely chopped
(1½ cups)

1 cup fresh unseeded rye bread
crumbs (2 slices, processed
into crumbs)

1 teaspoon salt

1 teaspoon ground allspice

¾ teaspoon freshly grated
nutmeg

½ teaspoon freshly ground
black pepper

1 pound very lean ground beef

½ pound ground turkey

⅓ cup nonfat (skim) milk

2 egg whites, lightly beaten

2 tablespoons unbleached
all-purpose flour

½ cup defatted beef or chicken
stock

1 cup 2% low-fat milk

The subtle flavor of these tasty meatballs is typical of Scandinavian dishes. I like to serve them with rye bread and applesauce.

1. Melt ½ tablespoon margarine in a large heavy skillet over low heat. Add the onion and cook, covered, until soft and translucent, about 10 minutes. Uncover and increase the heat to medium. Continue to cook the onion, stirring constantly, until lightly browned.

2. Spoon the cooked onion into a large bowl. (Do not wash the skillet.) To the onion mixture, add the bread crumbs, salt, ¾ teaspoon allspice, ½ teaspoon nutmeg, and ¼ teaspoon pepper and mix well. Add the beef, turkey, nonfat milk, and egg whites and mix thoroughly. Divide the mixture into thirty-six 1-ounce balls.

3. Heat the skillet used for the onion and brown the meatballs on all sides over medium heat. Reduce the heat to low and cook the meatballs, covered, for 10 more minutes.

4. While the meatballs are cooking, melt the remaining margarine in another pan over medium heat. Add the flour and cook, stirring constantly, for 2 minutes. Add the stock and remaining ¼ teaspoon allspice, ¼ teaspoon nutmeg, and ¼ teaspoon pepper and mix well. Slowly add the low-fat milk, stirring until slightly thickened. Remove the meatballs from the skillet with a slotted spoon and place them in the gravy. Reduce the heat to low and cook, covered, for another 10 minutes. Serve over noodles.

Makes 6 cups; six 1-cup servings

Each serving contains approximately:

Calories: 330   **Cholesterol: 85 mg**

Fat: 18 g   **Sodium: 615 mg**

Top: Swedish Meatballs,
page 99.

Left: Hoppin John,
page 102.

Finnish Venison Stew

4 cups water

1 teaspoon salt

1 teaspoon whole allspice

2 pounds venison, cut in 1-inch cubes, or top sirloin, all visible fat removed, cubed

1 medium onion, quartered

1 rutabaga (14 ounces), peeled and cubed (2½ cups)

1 celery root (1 pound), peeled and cubed (3½ cups)

3 medium carrots (8 ounces), peeled and sliced (1½ cups)

3 small parsnips (8 ounces), peeled and sliced (1½ cups)

4 small potatoes (1 pound), peeled and cubed (3 cups)

3 leeks, white part only, sliced (1½ cups)

Fresh parsley, for garnish

On a trip to Finland several years ago I had the pleasure of meeting their leading food writer, Anna-Maija Tanttu. She introduced me to many traditional Finnish dishes, which I found both uniquely different and absolutely delicious. One of my own favorites was their hearty vegetable and meat stew, which they more frequently call "soup." Finns make theirs with reindeer meat and leave the meat on the bone, but I prefer using boneless meat because it takes less time and creates less mess. Dark rye bread and mustard are perfect accompaniments for this dish. Though this recipe calls for venison or beef, it is also good made with any other meat, or you can omit the meat for a tasty vegetarian stew. If celery root is not available, replace it with diced celery.

1. In a large pot or soup kettle, combine the water, salt, and allspice and heat until warm. Add the meat and slowly bring to a simmer. Skim off any foam that appears on the surface. Add the onion and simmer, uncovered, for 20 minutes.

2. Add all the remaining vegetables, except the leeks and parsley, and cook, covered, over low heat for 1 hour. Add the leeks and cook another 15 minutes.

3. To serve, ladle the stew into bowls and garnish with parsley.

Makes about 16 cups; eight 2-cup servings

Each serving contains approximately:

Calories: 370	**Cholesterol: 77 mg**
Fat: 16 g	**Sodium: 420 mg**

Hoppin' John

1 medium onion, finely
    chopped (1½ cups)

1½ cups (6 ounces) diced
    Canadian bacon

2 cups (1 pound) dried
    black-eyed peas, soaked
    several hours or overnight

6 cups water or defatted
    chicken stock

1 teaspoon salt

¼ teaspoon freshly ground
    black pepper

¼ teaspoon red pepper flakes,
    or to taste

2 cups (14 ounces) uncooked
    long grain brown rice

3 cups canned ready-cut peeled
    tomatoes (1 28-ounce can)

1½ teaspoons liquid smoke

Since eating black-eyed peas on New Year's Day is supposed to ensure good luck throughout the coming year, it is a perfect time to treat your friends to a successful start. And what better way to serve them than from a bubbling caldron cooking over an open fire?

1. Cook the onion and bacon, covered, in a heavy pan or soup kettle over low heat until the onion is soft, about 10 minutes.

2. Drain and rinse the peas thoroughly and add to the onion and bacon mixture. Add the water, salt, pepper, and red pepper flakes and bring to a boil. Reduce to a simmer and cook, covered, for 45 minutes.

3. Add the rice and tomatoes, mix well, and continue to cook, covered, over low heat, for another 45 minutes. Check occasionally to be sure there is adequate liquid.

4. Add the liquid smoke and mix well. Serve on New Year's Day for good luck—or any other day of the year for good eatin'!

Makes 16 cups; twelve 1⅓-cup servings

Each serving contains approximately:

Calories: 300	**Cholesterol: 7 mg**
Fat: 3 g	**Sodium: 532 mg**

Olde English Cottage Pie

4 large russet potatoes, peeled
  and diced

3 tablespoons corn oil
  margarine

1 teaspoon salt

½ teaspoon freshly ground
  black pepper

½ cup nonfat (skim) milk

3 cups (12 ounces) grated 20%
  fat-reduced sharp cheddar
  cheese

1½ cups low-fat cottage cheese

1 medium onion, finely chopped
  (1½ cups)

2 medium carrots, grated or
  finely chopped (1½ cups)

1½ pounds lean ground round

4 cups (1 pound) sliced fresh
  mushrooms

¼ cup sherry

Paprika

1. Preheat the oven to 350°F. Boil the potatoes in a large pot until tender, about 10 minutes. Drain thoroughly and return to the pot. Add the margarine, ½ teaspoon salt, ¼ teaspoon pepper, the milk, and 1 cup grated cheese and mash thoroughly. Blend in the cottage cheese and again mix well. Set aside.

2. In a heavy skillet, cook the onion and carrots, covered, over low heat, until the onion is translucent, 10 to 15 minutes. Stir occasionally and add a little water, if necessary, to prevent scorching. Add the meat and cook, uncovered, stirring to keep the mixture crumbly. Add the remaining salt and pepper and mix well. Cook until the meat is no longer pink. Spoon the meat mixture into a colander lined with paper towels to absorb any grease.

3. Put the skillet back on the stove and add the mushrooms and sherry. Cook over medium heat, stirring occasionally, until the mushrooms are soft. Uncover and continue cooking until all of the sherry is absorbed, about 15 minutes.

4. To assemble, spread 2 cups of the mashed potato mixture in the bottom of a 3-quart flat baking dish that has been sprayed with nonstick vegetable coating. Spread the meat mixture evenly over the potatoes. Top with ¾ cup of the remaining cheese. Top the cheese with the mushrooms and top the mushrooms with the remaining potato mixture. Sprinkle the remaining cheese evenly over the top and lightly dust with paprika. Bake in the preheated oven for about 40 minutes or until the top is nicely browned. Allow to stand 10 to 15 minutes before serving.

Makes eight 1½-cup servings

Each serving contains approximately:

Calories: 480	**Cholesterol: 96 mg**
Fat: 21 g	**Sodium: 738 mg**

Green Eggs and Ham
en Croustade

1 large round loaf
   whole-grain bread, unsliced

3 tablespoons extra-virgin
   olive oil

8 egg whites

½ cup nonfat (skim) milk

½ cup chopped fresh parsley

½ teaspoon fresh or dried
   rosemary leaves

½ teaspoon dried thyme,
   crushed with a mortar and
   pestle

¼ teaspoon salt, or ⅛
   teaspoon if using liquid egg
   substitute

½ teaspoon freshly ground
   black pepper

8 whole eggs, or 2 cups liquid
   egg substitute

This version of Green Eggs and Ham en Croustade is the most unusual and elegant presentation of this classic combination I could dream up in memory of my treasured friend and mentor, Dr. Seuss. When you taste it, I hope you will agree with the absurdly wonderful Seussian character who, after finally agreeing to try something new, exclaims:

"I do so like Green Eggs and Ham!
Thank you! Thank you, Sam-I-Am."

If you want to eliminate the cholesterol from the whole eggs in this recipe, I have provided the option of using a liquid egg substitute. Also, the nutritional information assumes that only the lid of the croustade "bowl" will be eaten.

1. Preheat the oven to 325°F. Slice the top off the loaf of bread. To make the croustade, carefully hollow out the loaf, leaving walls ¾ inch thick. (Save the bread crumbs to use in other recipes.)

2. Using a pastry brush, evenly apply 2 tablespoons olive oil to the entire inner surface of the croustade and the cut side of the lid. Place the croustade "bowl" and lid, cut side up, in the preheated oven for about 25 to 30 minutes or until it is well toasted. Remove to a serving platter and keep warm.

3. While the croustade is toasting, beat the egg whites in a large mixing bowl until they form soft peaks and set aside. In a blender, combine the milk, parsley, rosemary, thyme, salt, and pepper. Cover and blend until smooth. Turn off the blender and add the eggs or egg substitute. Cover and blend again until the eggs are completely combined with the "green mixture." Pour the blender mixture into the bowl with the egg whites and fold in the whites until no streaks of white show.

4. Heat the remaining tablespoon of olive oil in a large nonstick skillet over medium-high heat. Add the garlic and cook just until it sizzles. Add the Parmesan cheese and the egg mixture, then

1 garlic clove, pressed or minced (1 teaspoon)

1 cup (4 ounces) grated Parmesan cheese

6 ounces cooked extra-lean ham, chopped

1 tablespoon finely chopped fresh parsley, for garnish

Parsley or sprigs of fresh rosemary, for garnish

reduce the heat to medium and stir the eggs constantly until they are almost set. Add the chopped ham and cook until the eggs are the desired consistency. Be careful not to overcook the eggs—it makes them too dry.

5. Remove the eggs from the heat and spoon them into the warm, toasted croustade on the serving platter. Sprinkle the chopped parsley over the top of the eggs and decorate the platter with parsley or sprigs of fresh rosemary. To serve, spoon the Green Eggs and Ham onto plates and cut the lid into six pie-shaped wedges to go with it.

Makes six ¾-cup servings

Each serving contains approximately:

Calories: 369   **Cholesterol: 309 mg**

Fat: 21 g   **Sodium: 1,170 mg**

With egg substitute each serving contains approximately:

Calories: 340   **Cholesterol: 26 mg**

Fat: 17g   **Sodium: 1,137 mg**

Green Eggs and Ham en Croustade.

Cassoulet Provençal

1 cup dried small white beans

1 pound lamb shoulder chops,
   with bones

1 medium onion, coarsely
   chopped

2 tomatoes, peeled, seeded, and
   chopped

6 garlic cloves, minced or
   pressed

4 teaspoons dried thyme,
   crushed with a mortar and
   pestle

1½ cups dry white wine

1½ cups water

2 tablespoons white vinegar

1 teaspoon salt

A cassoulet is really the French way of using up all of the week's leftovers, combining them with white beans and cooking them long enough for the flavors to "marry." For the purposes of this recipe, I am assuming that you don't have any leftovers in your refrigerator, so I have included a lamb stew recipe, to be made the day before, as well as instructions for cooking the chicken in the recipe. If you do have leftovers, such as stew or cooked poultry, by all means use them.

1. The day before serving, soak the beans and make the lamb stew. Put the beans in a bowl and add enough water to cover by several inches. Set aside to soak overnight.

2. To make the stew, remove all visible fat from the lamb, separate the bones from the meat, and cut the meat into bite-size pieces. Cook the lamb with the bones and the coarsely chopped onion in a large, heavy pot over medium heat for 10 minutes, stirring frequently. Add the tomatoes, garlic, and 2 teaspoons thyme. Pour in the wine, water, and vinegar and season with salt and pepper. Bring to a boil, then reduce the heat and simmer for 1 hour.

3. Strain the liquid (lamb stock) and let it cool to room temperature. Refrigerate the stock, uncovered, and transfer the lamb and vegetables to a bowl. Remove the bones and discard them. Cover and refrigerate the lamb and vegetables.

4. The next day, remove the fat from the top of the stock and bring the stock to a boil in a large pot. Drain and rinse the soaked beans and add them to the boiling stock, along with the finely chopped onion, carrots, celery, rosemary, bay leaves, parsley, and peppercorns. If necessary, add enough water to cover by 1 inch. Simmer, covered, for 1 hour, or until the beans are tender, adding more water if necessary.

1 teaspoon freshly ground black pepper

1 medium onion, finely chopped

2 small carrots, peeled and diced

1 stalk celery, diced

¼ teaspoon fresh or dried rosemary leaves

3 bay leaves

¼ cup chopped fresh parsley

10 peppercorns

4 chicken thighs, boned, skinned, and halved

1 cup fresh whole wheat bread crumbs

1 tablespoon corn oil margarine, melted

5. Preheat the oven to 325°F. Place the halved chicken thighs on a roasting pan. Sprinkle the remaining 2 teaspoons thyme on the chicken thighs and roast the chicken for 15 minutes. Remove from the oven and reduce the oven temperature to 300°F.

6. To assemble the cassoulet, drain the bean mixture, reserving the liquid. Remove and discard the bay leaves. In a deep 3-quart casserole, layer half the beans, then the lamb and vegetable mixture, and then the chicken thighs. Cover with the remaining bean mixture. Pour 1 cup of the reserved cooking liquid from the beans over the top.

7. Combine the bread crumbs and melted margarine and mix thoroughly. Sprinkle over the top of the casserole and bake for 1½ hours.

Makes about 9 cups; six 1½-cup servings

Each serving contains approximately:

Calories: 410   **Cholesterol: 60 mg**

Fat: 20 g   **Sodium: 660 mg**

Rabbit in Mustard Sauce

½ teaspoon salt

½ teaspoon freshly ground black pepper

2 tablespoons extra-virgin olive oil

2 medium onions, coarsely chopped (3 cups)

2 cups (8 ounces) sliced fresh mushrooms

½ cup Dijon mustard

1½ teaspoons dried thyme, crushed with a mortar and pestle

2 cups dry white wine

½ cup fresh bread crumbs

8 ounces dry eggless noodles

Fresh thyme leaves, for garnish (optional)

Sprigs of fresh thyme, for garnish (optional)

In France rabbit stew is one of the most popular bistro dishes. My favorite of these rabbit dishes is always the one with the most mustard. With this in mind, I developed this rabbit recipe—which may appeal only to those who share my passion for Dijon mustard.

1 fresh 2½-pound rabbit, cut into 8 pieces

1. Trim all visible fat from the rabbit and sprinkle with the salt and pepper.

2. Heat 1 tablespoon oil in a large pot or Dutch oven over medium-high heat until water dances on the surface. Add the rabbit pieces and brown well on both sides. Remove the rabbit to a bowl and set aside. Do not wash the pot.

3. In the same pot, cook the onions until brown. Add the mushrooms and cook until soft. Add the mustard, thyme, and wine and mix well. Bring to a boil, then reduce to a simmer and add the rabbit pieces. Cook, covered, for 30 minutes, or until the rabbit is completely tender.

4. Remove the rabbit to a warm platter. Bring the sauce back to a boil and add the bread crumbs. Cook, stirring constantly, until slightly thickened, about 3 minutes.

5. Meanwhile, cook the noodles al dente. Drain thoroughly and toss with the remaining tablespoon of oil. To serve, place 1 cup noodles on each of four plates and top with 2 pieces of rabbit. Cover with 1 cup sauce and garnish with thyme leaves and sprigs, if desired. (Or return the rabbit to the sauce and serve like a stew over the noodles.)

Makes 4 servings

Each serving contains approximately:

Calories: 565

Fat: 17 g

Cholesterol: 65 mg

Sodium: 828 mg

Top: Rabbit in Mustard Sauce.

Gingered Beef Stir-fry on Sesame Chuka Soba Noodles, page 110.

Gingered Beef Stir-fry on Sesame Chuka Soba Noodles

2 tablespoons sodium-reduced
  soy sauce

2 tablespoons sherry

2 teaspoons sugar

1 tablespoon peeled and
  minced fresh ginger root

3 garlic cloves, minced
  (1 tablespoon)

1 pound flank steak, all
  visible fat removed and cut
  with the grain into 1/4-inch-
  thick strips

4 teaspoons rice vinegar

2 teaspoons cornstarch

2 tablespoons dark sesame oil

4 green onions, cut diagonally
  into 3-inch pieces

1 cup (1/4 pound) thinly
  sliced fresh mushrooms

1/4 pound fresh snow pea pods,
  strings removed and pods
  notched at each end

1 red bell pepper, seeds and
  membranes removed, cut
  lengthwise into thin strips
  (1 cup)

2 cups cubed fresh pineapple

12 ounces dry Chuka Soba
  noodles

When making this dish it is important to get the wok or skillet very hot so that you end up with a stir-fry rather than a stew. Also remember to stir it constantly while cooking and remove the vegetables while they are still crisp-tender and colorful.

Chuka Soba noodles are available in most supermarkets and all Asian markets.

1. In a shallow pan, combine the soy sauce, sherry, sugar, ginger, and garlic and mix well. Add the meat strips and mix until the meat is well coated. Allow to marinate for at least 1 hour.

2. Remove the meat from the marinade and set aside. To the marinade add the rice vinegar and cornstarch and stir until the cornstarch is completely dissolved. Set aside.

3. Heat a wok or large heavy skillet until hot. Add 1 tablespoon of the oil and the steak and stir-fry over medium-high heat for 2 minutes. Add the vegetables, pineapple, and marinade mixture and stir-fry for about 3 more minutes or until the vegetables are crisp-tender.

4. Cook the noodles in rapidly boiling water for 2 minutes. Drain well and toss with the remaining tablespoon of oil. To serve, place 1 cup noodles in a ring on each of four plates. Top with 2 cups of the beef mixture.

Makes 4 servings

Each serving contains approximately:

Calories: 570	**Cholesterol: 61 mg**
Fat: 22g	**Sodium: 367 mg**

Cantonese Sweet-and-Sour Pork

1 tablespoon peanut or canola
oil

1 pound pork loin, all visible
fat removed, cut in 1-inch
cubes

1 20-ounce can pineapple
chunks, packed in natural
juice

2 tablespoons cornstarch

½ teaspoon salt

½ cup rice vinegar

3 tablespoons sugar

1 tablespoon sodium-reduced
soy sauce

½ large onion, thinly sliced
(1 cup)

1 red bell pepper, seeds and
membranes removed, thinly
sliced

1½ cups (6 ounces) sliced fresh
mushrooms

½ cup snow pea pods, strings
removed, pods notched at the
ends

1 8-ounce can water chestnuts,
drained and sliced

6 cups cooked rice

This is a wonderful dish to serve for a Chinese theme party. The preparation is relatively easy and it cooks in minutes. All you need are plates and chopsticks for serving, and fortune cookies make a great dessert.

1. Heat the oil in a large wok or skillet over medium-high heat. Add the pork and cook, stirring constantly, until the pork is no longer pink. Remove the pork from the pan and drain in a colander lined with paper towels and set aside.

2. Drain the juice from the pineapple into the wok or skillet and set the pineapple aside. To the juice add the cornstarch, salt, and vinegar, and stir until the cornstarch has completely dissolved. Heat the mixture over medium heat, stirring frequently, until it comes to a boil and thickens. Stir in the sugar, soy sauce, pork, and pineapple. Mix well, remove from the heat, and allow to marinate for 30 minutes.

3. Bring the mixture back to a boil over medium-high heat and add all the remaining ingredients except the rice. Cook, stirring constantly, until the vegetables are crisp-tender, about 2 to 3 minutes. To serve, spoon 1 cup of the mixture over 1 cup cooked rice, or serve the rice in a bowl on the side.

Makes 6 servings

Each serving contains approximately:

Calories: 560   **Cholesterol: 54 mg**

Fat: 12 g   **Sodium: 352 mg**

Peanut Butter Waffles, page 118.

Fruit Bran Muffins

Aebleskivers
(Pancake Balls)

Baked Apple Pancake

Corn and Cherry Cakes

breads

Peanut Butter Waffles

Apple Butter

Breakfast Cheese

&

Chocolate Quick Bread

break-

Baked French Toast

Full of Corn Sticks

fast

Raspberry-Almond Cheese Coffee Cake

Buckwheat Blinis

Blueberry Buckle

Quick Anise Biscotti

Fruit Bran Muffins

2 cups uncooked old-fashioned
  oatmeal

2 cups boiling water

8 egg whites

¾ cup canola or corn oil

1 cup sugar

1 teaspoon salt

4 cups buttermilk

3 cups whole wheat flour

5 teaspoons baking soda

4 cups unprocessed wheat bran

¼ cup dried fruit for each 1
  cup batter (optional)

This is a recipe I developed for the Peninsula Hotel in New York where it was served in their luxurious urban spa for early morning exercisers. It was so popular that it is now also available in their dining room and for room service, as well.

1. In a large mixing bowl, combine the oatmeal and boiling water, mix well, and set aside.

2. In a separate bowl, combine the egg whites, oil, sugar, salt, and buttermilk and mix well.

3. Add the liquid ingredients to the oatmeal mixture and mix well. Add the remaining dry ingredients and mix until just moistened. Do not overmix. Store, tightly covered, in the refrigerator. It will keep for up to three weeks.

4. To make the muffins, measure the amount of batter needed for the number of muffins to be made. Add ¼ cup *dried* fruit—raisins, dates, cherries, blueberries, bananas, pineapple, apricots, prunes, etc.—to each 1 cup batter, if desired. Fill muffin tins that have been sprayed with nonstick vegetable coating with batter (¼ cup each for standard muffins) and bake in a preheated 400°F. oven for 20 minutes.

Makes 12 cups batter; forty-eight ¼-cup muffins

Each muffin contains approximately:

Calories: 107	**Cholesterol: 1 mg**
Fat: 4 g	**Sodium: 166 mg**

Aebleskivers

(Pancake Balls)

1 cup whole wheat flour

1 cup unbleached all-purpose
 flour

2 teaspoons baking powder

½ teaspoon baking soda

½ teaspoon salt

2 tablespoons sugar

2 cups buttermilk

1 whole egg, separated

2 egg whites

3 tablespoons melted margarine

These Danish pancake balls are made in heavy aebleskiver pans that have cup-shaped depressions which give the pancakes their round shape. Traditionally, Danish cooks use knitting needles to turn the pancakes over, but a fork works just as well. If you don't have an aebleskiver pan, cook the batter in a skillet or on a griddle just as you would cook any other pancakes, and turn them over with a spatula. Serve hot aebleskivers with applesauce, apple butter, fruit jam, or a dusting of confectioners' sugar.

1. Combine the flours, baking powder, baking soda, salt, and sugar and mix well.

2. Combine the buttermilk with the egg yolk and mix well. Beat the egg whites until firm peaks form and set aside.

3. Combine the dry ingredients plus 2 tablespoons of the melted margarine with the buttermilk mixture and mix well. Fold in the beaten egg whites.

4. Heat an aebleskiver pan or skillet until water dances on the surface before evaporating. Brush or wipe each cup or the skillet with a little of the remaining margarine and spoon 2 tablespoons batter into each cup or into the skillet for each pancake.

5. Cook until they start to get bubbly around the edge, then quickly turn them by piercing each ball with the tines of a fork or flipping them over in the skillet with a spatula. Continue cooking until the other side is lightly browned. Serve hot with applesauce, apple butter, jam, or a sprinkle of confectioners' sugar.

Makes about 24 aebleskivers; 24 servings

Each serving contains approximately:

Calories: 65	**Cholesterol: 10 mg**
Fat: 2 g	**Sodium: 168 mg**

Baked Apple Pancake

1 tablespoon corn oil
    margarine

2 large or 3 small apples,
    peeled and thinly sliced
    (4 cups)

2 eggs, separated

¾ cup nonfat (skim) milk

½ teaspoon vanilla extract

1 egg white

2 tablespoons packed dark
    brown sugar, pushed through
    a sieve

½ teaspoon ground cinnamon

¼ teaspoon salt

½ cup plus 1 tablespoon
    unbleached all-purpose flour

¾ teaspoon baking powder

I particularly like this pancake recipe because you don't have to keep pouring batter on a griddle and then watch it carefully to be sure you don't overbrown the pancakes. I also use this recipe for dessert and serve it warm with a dollop of either low-fat vanilla ice cream or frozen yogurt.

1. Preheat the oven to 425°F. Melt the margarine in the oven in a 10-inch pie plate, quiche dish, or ovenproof skillet. Remove from the oven and add the apple slices. Return to the oven and bake for about 20 minutes, or until the apples are slightly cooked.

2. While the apples are cooking, combine the egg yolks, milk, and vanilla, mix well, and set aside. In a separate bowl, beat the egg whites just until they form soft peaks. In another bowl, sift together the brown sugar, cinnamon, salt, flour, and baking powder and mix well.

3. Pour the milk mixture all at once into the dry ingredients, mixing just until moistened. The batter will be lumpy. Fold in the egg whites.

4. Pour the batter over the apples and bake until well browned and puffed, about 20 to 25 minutes. Cut into 6 wedges and serve immediately.

Makes 6 servings

Each serving contains approximately:

Calories: 159   **Cholesterol: 72 mg**

Fat: 4 g   **Sodium: 252 mg**

Baked Apple Pancakes.

Corn and Cherry Cakes

½ cup yellow cornmeal

½ cup whole wheat flour

¾ teaspoon baking powder

½ teaspoon salt

¼ cup sugar

1 cup corn kernels (use 2 ears
   lightly steamed; or frozen
   corn, thawed)

½ cup chopped dried cherries

1 cup nonfat (skim) milk

2 egg whites

1 tablespoon corn or canola oil

¼ cup (1 ounce) low-fat cottage
   cheese

*Bottom left: Aebleskivers,
page 115.*

*Middle: Blueberry Buckle,
page 126.*

*Bottom right: Corn and
Cherry Cakes.*

*Try making silver dollar–sized corn cakes for breakfast or teatime.
They are good served alone or with a bit of low-fat ricotta cheese or light
cream cheese spread on the top.*

1. Combine the cornmeal, flour, baking powder, salt, and sugar
and stir until well mixed. Add the corn and cherries and stir until
well mixed.

2. Combine the milk, egg whites, and oil in a blender and blend
on medium speed until well mixed. Pour into the dry ingredients,
add the cottage cheese, and stir just until the dry ingredients are
evenly moistened. Allow the batter to rest for 15 minutes.

3. To cook, heat a nonstick skillet or griddle over medium heat
until drops of water sprinkled on the surface dance around before
evaporating. For each corn cake, spoon 2 tablespoons batter onto
the hot surface and cook about 2 minutes per side, or until a rich
golden brown.

Makes 3 cups batter; about 24 corn cakes

Each cake contains approximately:

Calories: 55   **Cholesterol: Negligible**

Fat: 1 g   **Sodium: 90 mg**

Peanut Butter Waffles

1½ cups whole wheat flour

¾ cup uncooked quick-cooking
   oatmeal

1 tablespoon baking powder

½ teaspoon salt

¾ cup unhomogenized crunchy
   peanut butter

1 tablespoon dark sesame oil

¼ cup sugar

¼ cup packed dark brown
   sugar

2 egg whites, lightly beaten

2 cups nonfat (skim) milk

2 teaspoons vanilla extract

I first developed Gingerbread Pancakes for the La Valencia Hotel in La Jolla, and they almost immediately became the best-selling item on the breakfast menu. So when their food and beverage manager asked me to come up with another breakfast item to compete with them, I tried to think of something I like as much as gingerbread and I immediately thought of peanut butter. I didn't want another pancake, so I started working on a waffle. The trick was to achieve a strong peanut-butter flavor without an outrageous amount of fat. I finally decided that this recipe was as pure as I could get it without sacrificing taste and texture. It is served with Apple Butter and Breakfast Cheese (both on opposite page), which is a sublimely flavorful combination, and it brings the percentage of calories from fat down to an acceptable 30 percent.

1. Preheat a waffle iron and spray it with nonstick vegetable coating. In a large mixing bowl, combine the flour, oatmeal, baking powder, and salt and mix well.

2. In another bowl, combine the peanut butter, oil, and sugars and mix until completely blended. Add the egg whites and mix well. Add the milk, a little at a time, blending well after each addition. Add the vanilla and again mix well.

3. Pour the liquid into the dry ingredients and mix just until the dry ingredients are moistened. Do not overmix. Immediately spoon ½ cup batter into the preheated waffle iron and bake for about 7 minutes, or until golden brown and the waffle stops steaming.

Makes 8 waffles

Each waffle contains approximately:

Calories: 340	**Cholesterol: 1 mg**
Fat: 15 g	**Sodium: 450 mg**

Apple Butter

2 cups dried, sliced, unsulfured
   apples
1 teaspoon ground cinnamon
½ teaspoon ground allspice
⅛ teaspoon ground cloves
2 cups unsweetened apple juice

1. Combine all ingredients in a large saucepan and bring to a boil over medium heat. Reduce heat to low, cover, and simmer for 20 minutes, stirring occasionally. Remove from heat and allow to cool to room temperature.

2. Pour into the work bowl of a food processor fitted with the steel blade or into a blender and blend until smooth. Refrigerate in a tightly covered container. It will keep for months.

Makes 2 cups; sixteen 2-tablespoon servings
Each serving contains approximately:

Calories: 35   **Cholesterol: None**
Fat: Negligible   **Sodium: 5 mg**

Breakfast Cheese

1 cup part-skim ricotta cheese
2 tablespoons plain nonfat
   yogurt

1. Combine the cheese and yogurt in a bowl and mix with a whisk until smooth, or process in a food processor or blender.

2. Refrigerate in a tightly covered container. The fresher your ingredients, the longer it will keep.

Makes about 1 cup; eight 2-tablespoon servings
Each serving contains approximately:

Calories: 40   **Cholesterol: 9 mg**
Fat: 2 g   **Sodium: 38 mg**

Chocolate Quick Bread

2 cups unbleached all-purpose
  flour

½ cup unsweetened dry cocoa
  powder

½ cup sugar

1½ teaspoons baking powder

1½ teaspoons baking soda

½ teaspoon salt

1 teaspoon ground cinnamon

1 teaspoon instant coffee

¼ cup boiling water

1 egg, lightly beaten

¼ cup canola or corn oil

1 cup nonfat (skim) milk

2 tablespoons white vinegar

1 tablespoon vanilla extract

If you love to bake bread but hate kneading it, this recipe should please you enormously. It's quick, it's easy, and it is so delicious that your family and friends will beg you for the recipe. For a real chocolate indulgence try making finger sandwiches out of this Chocolate Quick Bread, spreading it with peanut butter, and serving it with cocoa.

1. Preheat the oven to 350°F. Spray a standard-size loaf pan with nonstick vegetable coating.

2. In a large bowl, combine the flour, cocoa, sugar, baking powder, baking soda, salt, and cinnamon and mix well. In a small bowl, combine the instant coffee and boiling water and stir to dissolve.

3. In another bowl, combine the egg and oil and mix well. Add the milk, vinegar, vanilla, and the coffee mixture and mix well.

4. Add the liquid ingredients to the dry ingredients and mix just until the dry ingredients are moistened. Do not overmix. Spoon into the prepared pan and bake for 55 to 60 minutes, or until a knife inserted in the center comes out clean. Cool for 15 minutes in the pan on a rack. Remove from the pan and cool completely before slicing. Store, tightly wrapped, in the refrigerator.

Makes 1 loaf; 16 slices

Each slice contains approximately:

Calories: 130

Fat: 5 g

Cholesterol: 14 mg

Sodium: 175 mg

Chocolate Quick Bread.

Baked French Toast

10 slices whole wheat bread

1½ cups (1 12-ounce can)
  canned evaporated skim milk

2 eggs

4 egg whites

⅓ cup packed dark brown
  sugar

1 teaspoon vanilla extract

½ teaspoon ground cinnamon

Nonstick vegetable coating

Whenever I have overnight house guests this is the recipe I fall back on for breakfast. I make it the night before and all I have to do in the morning is put it in the oven.

For a fancier presentation, layer the bread in a round casserole or quiche dish and slice into pie-shaped wedges to serve. (If you desire, 1 cup liquid egg substitute may be used instead of the 2 eggs and 4 egg whites in this recipe.)

1. Lightly spray a 9 x 13 x 2-inch pan with nonstick vegetable coating. Arrange the bread slices in the bottom of the pan (it will be a snug fit).

2. Combine all the remaining ingredients and mix well using a whisk or egg beater. Pour the mixture evenly over the bread, cover tightly, and refrigerate several hours or overnight.

3. To bake, preheat the oven to 350°F. Remove the bread from the refrigerator and spray lightly with nonstick vegetable coating. Bake in the preheated oven for 30 to 35 minutes, or until lightly browned.

Makes 10 single-slice servings

Each slice contains approximately:

Calories: 136   **Cholesterol: 45 mg**

Fat: 2 g   **Sodium: 201 mg**

Baked French Toast.

Full of Corn Sticks

¾ cup yellow cornmeal

¾ cup unbleached all-purpose flour

1 tablespoon baking powder

½ teaspoon salt

2 tablespoons sugar

½ cup steamed fresh corn kernels (1 ear corn)

2 egg whites

2 tablespoons corn or canola oil

1 cup grated fresh corn (2 to 3 ears corn)

I developed these tasty, dairy-free corn sticks for Cooking Light *magazine and they are truly just as "corny" as they can be! This recipe is really good when it is made with fresh corn. Of course, you can substitute frozen corn kernels—but my advice is to make these corn sticks in the summertime when fresh corn is readily available.*

1. Preheat the oven to 425°F. Combine the cornmeal, flour, baking powder, salt, and sugar in a bowl and stir until well mixed. Stir in the steamed corn kernels until well mixed.

2. In a blender, combine the egg whites, oil, and grated corn and blend on medium speed until smooth. Pour the liquid into the dry ingredients and stir just until all the dry ingredients are moistened.

3. Spray cast-iron corn stick molds (see Note) with nonstick vegetable coating. Spoon ¼ cup batter into each mold and bake 15 minutes in the preheated oven, or until a golden brown. Remove from the oven and place on a rack to cool slightly before removing from the molds. If you have only one mold, you will have to repeat this process. Serve warm. If reheating, wrap in foil and place in a preheated 350°F. oven for about 10 minutes.

Makes 12 sticks

Each stick contains approximately:

Calories: 85   **Cholesterol: None**

Fat: 1 g   **Sodium: 280 mg**

Note: If you don't have a cast-iron corn stick mold, use a regular muffin tin, custard cups, or small ramekins.

Raspberry-Almond Cheese Coffee Cake

2½ cups unbleached
  all-purpose flour

¾ cup sugar

½ cup corn oil margarine

½ teaspoon baking powder

½ teaspoon baking soda

¼ teaspoon salt

1 cup light sour cream

1 teaspoon almond extract

4 egg whites

8 ounces Neufchâtel cheese,
  softened

½ cup fruit-only raspberry
  preserves

¼ cup sliced almonds

Rather than calling this remarkably tasty coffee cake "light," I prefer to call it "lighter." Even though it hardly meets the nutritional profile for a spa menu, it is certainly less sinful than the original recipe which had almost double the calories and fat. To cut the calories and fat substantially, just eat half a piece.

1. Preheat the oven to 350°F. Spray the bottom and sides of a 9- or 10-inch springform pan with nonstick vegetable coating. In a large bowl combine the flour and ½ cup of the sugar. Using a pastry blender or fork, cut in the margarine until the mixture resembles coarse crumbs. Reserve 1 cup of the crumb mixture.

2. To the remaining crumb mixture, add the baking powder, baking soda, salt, sour cream, almond extract, and 2 of the egg whites and blend well. Spread the batter over the bottom and 2 inches up the sides of the prepared pan. The batter should be about ¼ inch thick on the sides.

3. In a small bowl, combine the cheese, remaining ¼ cup sugar, and remaining 2 egg whites and blend well. Pour into the batter-lined pan. Carefully spoon the preserves evenly over the cheese mixture.

4. In another small bowl, combine the reserved crumb mixture and sliced almonds and sprinkle over the preserves. Bake in the preheated oven 45 to 50 minutes, or until the cheese is set and the crust is deep golden brown. Cool 15 minutes, then remove the sides of the pan. This cake may be served warm or cool. Store, tightly covered, in the refrigerator.

Makes 12 servings

Each serving contains approximately:

Calories: 233	**Cholesterol: 22 mg**
Fat: 16 g	**Sodium: 318 mg**

Buckwheat Blinis

½ cup plus 1 tablespoon whole wheat flour

½ cup plus 1 tablespoon buckwheat flour

1 package (1 tablespoon) active dry yeast (check date on package before using)

2 egg yolks

1½ cups nonfat (skim) milk, warmed

4 egg whites, beaten until stiff

2 tablespoons corn oil margarine, melted

Every time I make these puffy little pancakes, I remember the first time I tasted them. I was sitting, looking out over Hong Kong Harbor from the top of the Mandarin Oriental Hotel, in the only Petrossian Caviar restaurant in Asia. The blinis were served with a combination of beluga, sevruga, and osetra caviar in a sterling silver and glass presentoir with gold palette knives for spreading the caviar on the blinis. The captain explained that gold is one of the few metals that doesn't affect the taste of caviar. I will add to his comment that, in my opinion, Buckwheat Blinis are the only bread I like to serve with fine caviar and that if you serve lots of blinis and a small amount of caviar, the precious little sturgeon eggs are much more affordable! I also like a little light sour cream with my blinis and caviar.

1. Combine the flours and yeast and mix well. Add the egg yolks and milk and again mix well. Fold in the egg whites and melted margarine.

2. To cook, heat a griddle or heavy skillet over medium heat. Oil the surface and wipe dry. For each blini, spoon 1 tablespoon batter onto the hot surface and cook until bubbles form and break. Turn over and lightly brown on the other side.

Makes six cups batter; about 90 blinis

Each blini contains approximately:

Calories: 12	**Cholesterol: 6 mg**
Fat: Negligible	**Sodium: 8 mg**

Blueberry Buckle

2 tablespoons corn oil margarine, softened

½ cup sugar

2 egg whites

½ cup nonfat (skim) milk

½ cup unsweetened applesauce

2 cups unbleached all-purpose
  flour

2½ teaspoons baking powder

¼ teaspoon salt

2 cups fresh blueberries

topping:

¼ cup sugar

¼ cup unbleached all-purpose
  flour

½ teaspoon ground cinnamon

1 tablespoon corn oil
  margarine

This is a recipe I revised for my column. I called my revision "Buckle Tightening" because I was able to drop the calories from 308 to 180 and the grams of fat from 14 to 3 without losing the taste or texture of this moist and delicious coffee cake.

1. Preheat the oven to 350°F. Thoroughly cream the margarine and sugar. Add the egg whites, milk, and applesauce and blend well.

2. In a separate bowl, combine the flour, baking powder, and salt. Add to the milk mixture and stir only until the dry ingredients are just moistened. Do not overmix. Spread the batter into an 11 x 7 x 1½-inch pan sprayed with nonstick vegetable coating and top with the berries.

3. To make the topping, combine the sugar, flour, and cinnamon. Cut in the margarine until crumbly and sprinkle over the berries. Bake in the preheated oven for 45 minutes. Cut into squares and serve warm.

Makes 12 servings

Each serving contains approximately:

Calories: 180   **Cholesterol: Negligible**

Fat: 3 g   **Sodium: 243 mg**

Quick Anise Biscotti

1 tablespoon corn oil
  margarine

¼ cup sugar

2 egg whites, lightly beaten

1 teaspoon anise extract

1 cup unbleached all-purpose
  flour

½ teaspoon baking powder

⅛ teaspoon salt

I love having biscotti on hand to serve with coffee. I particularly like it with espresso and cappuccino. After toasting these crunchy Italian cookies, allow them to come to room temperature and then store them in an airtight container—that is, if you can manage to save any after your family finds out you've made them.

1. Preheat the oven to 375°F. Combine the margarine and sugar and mix until completely blended. Add the egg whites and anise extract and mix well.

2. In another bowl, combine the flour, baking powder, and salt and mix well. Add the flour mixture to the sugar mixture and mix well.

3. Spoon the batter into a standard-size loaf pan that has been sprayed with nonstick vegetable coating. Spread evenly over the bottom of the pan by wetting your hand and pressing down on the dough. Place in the preheated oven and bake for 15 minutes, or until a knife inserted in the center comes out clean.

4. Remove from the oven and turn onto a cutting surface. Just as soon as the loaf is cool enough to handle, cut it into sixteen ½-inch slices. Place the slices on a baking sheet that is either covered with parchment paper or that has been sprayed with nonstick vegetable coating and bake for 5 minutes. Turn the slices over and bake for 5 more minutes, or until a golden brown on both sides.

Makes sixteen 1-slice servings

Calories: 48   **Cholesterol: None**

Fat: 2 g   **Sodium: 56 mg**

Poached Pear Gratin and Sparkling Apple-Pear Cider, page 134.

Baked Apple Cups

Christmas Mincemeat Cream with Rum Sauce

Golden Apple Brown Betty

Holiday Pudding with Brandy Sauce

Brandy Sauce

dessert

Poached Pear Gratin and Sparkling Apple-Pear Cider

Sparkling Apple-Pear Cider

Southern Poached Pears with Gentleman Jack Sauce

Lemon Meringue Pie

Pie Crust

Fresh Pineapple Upside-down Cake

"Prudent" Pumpkin Pie

Apple Tarte Tatin

Baked Apple Cups

4 Golden Delicious apples,
   cored and halved lengthwise

2 large lemons

3 tablespoons sugar

2 Granny Smith apples

2 cups melted vanilla ice milk

Mint leaves for garnish,
   (optional)

This apple dessert tastes amazingly rich to be so low in calories and cholesterol. The secret is using melted vanilla ice milk as the sauce instead of a classic crème anglaise, which is made with egg yolks.

1. Preheat the oven to 350°F. Place the apples in a large baking dish, cut side up, and bake until easily pierced with a fork, 30 to 40 minutes. Remove from the oven and set aside. Leave the oven on.

2. Peel the lemons, being careful to cut off only the yellow outside part of the peel. Cut the peel in thin matchstick-size strips. Place the strips in a saucepan, cover with water, and bring to a boil. Boil for 2 minutes, then drain and set aside. Juice the peeled lemons and combine with the sugar in a large bowl, mix well, and set aside.

3. Core and peel the Granny Smith apples, then cut them in thin matchstick-size strips. Combine them with the lemon peel, then stir them into the juice-and-sugar mixture, mix well, and set aside.

4. Make cups out of the baked Golden Delicious apple halves by using a spoon to carefully remove all but about ¼ inch of the pulp from the skin. Be careful not to tear the skin. Then, cut the pulp in thin matchstick-size strips and mix it well with the apple-lemon mixture.

5. Fill each apple cup with ½ cup apple mixture and pour any remaining juice evenly over each serving. Return to the oven until the apple filling is crisp-tender, about 20 minutes, then place the apple cups on a large plate to cool. Pour any pan juices evenly over each serving. When cool, cover and refrigerate until cold.

6. To serve, place each apple cup on a plate. Pour ¼ cup melted ice milk over the top of each cup. Garnish with mint leaves.

Makes 8 servings

Each serving contains approximately:

Calories: 130	Cholesterol: 5 mg
Fat: 2 g	Sodium: 28 mg

Christmas Mincemeat Cream with Rum Sauce

mousse:

1 9-ounce box mincemeat (I like Nonesuch)

2½ cups low-fat ricotta cheese

2 teaspoons vanilla extract

3 tablespoons brandy

sauce:

2 teaspoons cornstarch

¾ cup cool water

Dash of salt

3 tablespoons sugar

1½ tablespoons corn oil margarine

1 teaspoon vanilla extract

2 teaspoons dark rum

⅛ teaspoon nutmeg

Mincemeat pie is always a holiday favorite but it is so rich and high in calories that many families have taken it off their Thanksgiving and Christmas menus. If you've been forgoing this seasonal classic in favor of lighter fare, here's a recipe to put mincemeat back on your table. This mincemeat dessert is just as tasty and much lighter than old-fashioned mincemeat pie. It is also infinitely easier to make.

1. Combine all the mousse ingredients in a food processor fitted with the metal blade and blend until it has a smooth, creamy consistency. Be patient because this takes quite a while.

2. Store, covered, in the refrigerator several hours or overnight, before serving. It is best made a day in advance. (Makes 3 cups.)

3. To make the sauce, combine the cornstarch with ¼ cup of the water and stir until the cornstarch is completely dissolved.

4. Combine the salt, sugar, and remaining ½ cup water in a saucepan and bring to a boil. Add the cornstarch mixture and continue to cook over medium heat, stirring constantly for 5 minutes. Remove from the heat and add all remaining sauce ingredients, stirring until the margarine is melted. Allow the sauce to come to room temperature. Spoon 1 tablespoonful over each serving. (Makes ¾ cup sauce.)

Makes twelve ¼-cup servings

Each serving contains approximately:

Calories: 185	**Cholesterol: 16 mg**
Fat: 6 g	**Sodium: 183 mg**

Golden Apple Brown Betty

8 medium-size Golden
  Delicious apples, pared,
  cored, and thinly sliced
  (about 8 cups)

¾ cup frozen unsweetened
  apple juice concentrate,
  thawed and undiluted

½ cup raisins

½ cup plus 3 tablespoons
  whole wheat flour

1 teaspoon ground cinnamon

½ cup uncooked quick-cooking
  oatmeal

3 tablespoons packed dark
  brown sugar

3 tablespoons corn oil
  margarine, melted

*Below: Golden Apple
Brown Betty*

The secret of this recipe is using Golden Delicious apples rather than the Granny Smiths or pippins usually called for in old-fashioned Brown Betty recipes. They are much sweeter and therefore you can cut back on the sugar.

1. Preheat the oven to 350°F. In a large bowl, combine the apples, juice, raisins, 3 tablespoons flour, and cinnamon. Spoon into an 11 x 7 x 1½-inch baking dish.

2. Combine the oatmeal, ½ cup flour, and brown sugar. Stir in the melted margarine and mix until crumbly. Sprinkle over the apple mixture and bake in the preheated oven for 1 hour.

3. Remove from the oven and allow to cool slightly before serving. The mixture will be very moist with a little liquid remaining in the bottom of the baking dish. Spoon a little of the liquid over each serving.

Makes 6 cups; twelve ½-cup servings

Each serving contains approximately:

Calories: 206   **Cholesterol: None**

Fat: 5 g   **Sodium: 55 mg**

Holiday Pudding with Brandy Sauce

1 large yam (1 pound), grated
   (2 cups)

⅓ cup corn oil margarine,
   softened

1 cup whole wheat flour

½ cup packed dark brown
   sugar

1 cup raisins

6 ounces dried apricots,
   chopped (¾ cup packed)

½ teaspoon ground cinnamon

½ teaspoon freshly grated
   nutmeg

¼ teaspoon ground cloves

¼ teaspoon salt

2 tablespoons nonfat (skim)
   milk

½ teaspoon vinegar

½ teaspoon baking soda

1 cup Brandy Sauce
   (page 134)

Several years ago a reader sent me a recipe for her family's favorite holiday pudding. She wanted to get rid of the suet, because of the saturated fat, but didn't know what to substitute for it. I found that margarine worked beautifully and that I was able to use less of it. In fact, I was so happy with the "new" pudding, I served it with a brandy sauce for dessert at my own Christmas dinner. This is the easiest recipe for Brandy Sauce ever written and it's delicious on this Holiday Pudding.

1. Combine all the ingredients except the milk, vinegar, soda, and Brandy Sauce. Toss until thoroughly mixed.

2. Combine the milk and vinegar, then mix in the baking soda. Add to the other ingredients and toss thoroughly.

3. Cook, covered, on low heat over simmering water in the top of a 2½-quart double boiler that has been sprayed with nonstick vegetable coating for 3 hours, or until a knife inserted in the center comes out clean. Add more hot water to the bottom of the double boiler as needed.

4. To serve, spoon ½ cup pudding into each of eight dessert bowls and top with 2 tablespoons Brandy Sauce.

Makes eight ½-cup servings

Each serving contains approximately:

Calories: 400   **Cholesterol: 2 mg**

Fat: 9 g   **Sodium: 254 mg**

*Opposite right: Holiday
Pudding with Brandy Sauce.*

Brandy Sauce

1 cup melted vanilla ice milk

2 tablespoons brandy

Whisk the melted ice milk and brandy together, mixing well.

Makes 1 cup sauce; eight 2-tablespoon servings

Each serving contains approximately:

Calories: 35	**Cholesterol: 2 mg**
Fat: 1 g	**Sodium: 21 mg**

Poached Pear Gratin and Sparkling Apple-Pear Cider

8 Bartlett pears, peeled

4 cups apple cider

½ cup nonfat sour cream substitute

½ cup nonfat (skim) milk

¾ teaspoon vanilla extract

¼ cup packed dark brown sugar

Fresh mint, for garnish (optional)

This is a wonderful recipe because you end up with both a delightful dessert and a refreshing drink.

1. Place the peeled pears in a saucepan. Pour the apple cider over them and bring to a boil over medium heat. Reduce the heat and simmer just until the pears can be easily pierced with a fork. Remove from the heat and cool to room temperature. Cover and allow the pears to marinate in the apple cider for several hours or overnight in the refrigerator.

2. Remove the pears from the cider, reserving the cider to make the Sparkling Apple-Pear Cider (recipe follows). Remove the stems from the pears and cut each pear in half lengthwise. Carefully remove the seeds and core fiber from each pear half.

3. Place each pear half on a cutting board, cut side down. With a sharp knife starting about ½ inch from the stem end, make

slices in the pear all the way through to the opposite end and about ¼ inch apart. Fan the slices apart by pressing on them gently until the ends separate slightly. Arrange the fanned pears, cut side down, in a circular pattern in a quiche dish, or use individual gratin dishes and place 1 pear in each dish.

4. In a mixing bowl, whisk together the sour cream, milk, and vanilla until thoroughly mixed. Spoon the mixture over the pears.

5. Preheat the broiler. Just before broiling, sprinkle the brown sugar evenly over the pears, then broil the pears close to the heat source until the brown sugar melts and bubbles, about 1½ minutes. Serve warm. Garnish with fresh mint, if desired.

Makes 8 servings

Each serving contains approximately:

Calories: 145	**Cholesterol: Negligible**
Fat: 1 g	**Sodium: 22 mg**

Sparkling Apple-Pear Cider

3½ *cups cider, reserved from Poached Pear Gratin (opposite page), chilled*
2½ *cups cold sparkling water*

Combine the cider and sparkling water. Serve immediately.

Makes 6 cups; eight ¾-cup servings

Each serving contains approximately:

Calories: 60	**Cholesterol: None**
Fat: Negligible	**Sodium: 4 mg**

Southern Poached Pears
with Gentleman Jack Sauce

8 pears, with stems (Bartlett are best if available)

¼ cup packed dark brown sugar

¼ cup Gentleman Jack Rare Tennessee Whiskey (or Jack Daniels, or any bourbon)

¾ cup vanilla ice milk

Mint leaves, for garnish

The Jack Daniels distillery, located in Lynchburg, Tennessee, is a National Historical Landmark. A must in Lynchburg is dinner (called lunch up north) at Miss Mary Bobo's Boarding House. The dessert that was served the day I was there was so delicious I asked the proprietress, Miss Lynne Tolley, for her recipe. I must admit I have taken great license with the recipe she gave me, but I think you'll love this light, delicious, and beautiful southern-inspired dessert.

1. Carefully peel the pears, leaving the stems intact. Place them in a pot or saucepan large enough to hold all eight pears and cover with water. Add the brown sugar and slowly bring to a boil. Reduce the heat and simmer about 8 to 10 minutes, or until the pears can be easily pierced with a fork. Do not overcook or they will become mushy. Remove from the heat and allow to cool in the poaching liquid. Cover and refrigerate several hours or overnight.

2. Remove the pears from the liquid. Place the poaching liquid on the stove, bring to a boil, and boil until reduced in volume to 1 cup. When reduced, set aside and allow to cool.

3. While the liquid is reducing, halve the pears lengthwise, leaving the stems attached to one half of each pear. Carefully remove the core of each pear half, taking care to leave the pears intact. Set the six most attractive pears aside.

4. Remove the stems from the two remaining pears and place them in a blender container. Pour the reduced poaching liquid and Gentleman Jack into the container and puree until smooth. You should have about 2 cups puree. (At this point the pear halves and puree can be covered and refrigerated until ready to serve.)

Southern Poached Pears with Gentleman Jack Sauce.

5. To serve, divide half the puree equally among each of six plates, pouring a little on the bottom of each plate. Place a pear half with stem attached, cavity side down, on each plate on top of the puree. With a sharp knife, carefully make slices in the pear half, about ¼ inch apart and starting about ½ inch from the stem end. Fan the slices apart by pressing gently on them until they separate.

6. Place the remaining pear halves, cavity side up, next to each fanned pear half. Fill the cavity with a 1-ounce (2-tablespoon) ball of ice milk. Place a mint leaf beside each stem for garnish.

Makes 6 servings

Each serving contains approximately:

Calories: 210	**Cholesterol: 2 mg**
Fat: 2 g	**Sodium: 16 mg**

Lemon Meringue Pie

filling:

¾ cup sugar

3 tablespoons cornstarch

1 ½ cups cold water

2 egg yolks, lightly beaten

1 tablespoon corn oil
  margarine

1 tablespoon grated lemon
  rind

¼ cup fresh lemon juice

meringue:

3 egg whites

1 teaspoon fresh lemon juice

¼ cup sugar

1 baked 9-inch Pie Crust
  (recipe follows)

In this recipe, I use less sugar than is called for in most other lemon meringue pie recipes so the lemon flavor is a bit more pronounced. Also, even though I use only two egg yolks to reduce the cholesterol, the custard is just as smooth.

The California Egg Commission recommends that we keep eggs refrigerated at all times for health reasons. Therefore, I used four egg whites in the meringue to compensate for the volume lost by using cold egg whites. I also suggest cooking the pie on a baking sheet so that when you take the pie out of the oven, you don't get your potholders in the baked meringue.

1. Preheat the oven to 400°F. To make the filling, in a heavy 2-quart saucepan combine the sugar, cornstarch, and water and mix until the cornstarch is thoroughly dissolved. Add the egg yolks and mix thoroughly. Slowly bring to a boil over medium heat and allow to boil for 1 minute. Remove from the heat, add the margarine, and mix well. Add the grated lemon rind and lemon juice and again mix well. Set aside.

2. To make the meringue, combine the egg whites and lemon juice and, using an electric mixer, beat on high speed until foamy. Slowly add the sugar, 1 tablespoon at a time, beating until stiff peaks form and the sugar is completely dissolved. Do not overbeat.

3. To assemble the pie, spoon the warm custard into the pie shell and spread evenly. Spread the meringue evenly over the filling, being careful to seal it to the edge of the crust. Bake in the preheated oven for 8 to 10 minutes or until a golden brown. Allow to cool to room temperature away from a draft. May be served immediately or chilled before serving.

Makes 8 servings

Each serving contains approximately:

Calories: 240   **Cholesterol: 68 mg**

Fat: 7 g   **Sodium: 127 mg**

Pie Crust

1 cup unbleached all-purpose flour

⅛ teaspoon salt

3 tablespoons cold corn oil margarine

1 teaspoon fresh lemon juice

3 tablespoons ice water

1. Preheat the oven to 425°F. Combine the flour and salt in a large bowl and mix well. Add the margarine and cut into the flour mixture using two knives or a pastry blender until it looks like a coarse meal.

2. In a small bowl, combine the lemon juice and ice water and sprinkle over the dough, 1 tablespoon at a time, mixing with a fork or pastry blender. Form the dough into a ball and place on wax paper. Press the ball into a 4-inch circle and cover with another piece of wax paper.

3. Roll out the dough between the sheets of wax paper into a circle eleven inches in diameter. Remove the top piece of wax paper and, using the bottom paper, lift the crust and place in a 9-inch pie plate that has been sprayed with nonstick vegetable coating. Fold the edges under and flute.

4. To bake the pie shell, prick the bottom and sides of the dough with a fork to prevent buckling. Place in the center of the preheated oven and bake for 12 to 14 minutes, or until very lightly browned. May be filled immediately with lemon pie filling or placed on a rack to cool.

Makes one 9-inch crust; 8 servings

Each serving contains approximately:

Calories: 92	**Cholesterol: None**
Fat: 5 g	**Sodium: 88 mg**

Fresh Pineapple
Upside-down Cake

¼ cup chopped walnuts plus 1
  whole walnut half

2 tablespoons corn oil
  margarine

3 tablespoons dark brown
  sugar

1½ cups (1 12-ounce can)
  unsweetened frozen pineapple
  juice concentrate, thawed

1 4½-pound fresh pineapple,
  rind and core removed

1½ cups unbleached all-
  purpose flour

1 tablespoon baking powder

1 tablespoon ground cinnamon

½ teaspoon salt

3 egg whites

¼ cup canola or corn oil

1 tablespoon vanilla extract

When I was working on a fresh pineapple story for Cooking Light *magazine, I found that it is virtually impossible to use fresh pineapple without cooking it first because it contains an enzyme called bromelin that makes breads, cakes, and pie crusts soggy. However, this nasty trait works to great advantage in this fabulous Fresh Pineapple Upside-down Cake because it keeps the top moist.*

1. Preheat the oven to 350°F. Place the walnuts on a baking sheet and toast in the oven for 8 to 10 minutes, or until golden brown. Watch carefully because they burn easily. Set aside.

2. In a 10-inch heavy skillet, melt the margarine over low heat. Add the brown sugar and ¼ cup of the pineapple juice. Bring to a boil over low heat and simmer, stirring constantly, for 2 minutes. Remove from the heat.

3. Slice the pineapple into ¼-inch rings. Place one ring in the center of the skillet. Cut the remaining rings in half and arrange them around the central ring in a spoke pattern. Place the walnut half in the center of the pineapple ring and set the skillet aside.

4. Combine the flour, baking powder, cinnamon, and salt in a medium bowl and mix well. In another large bowl, beat the egg whites until soft peaks start to form. Continue beating while adding the remaining pineapple juice, the oil, and vanilla. Slowly beat in the dry ingredients. When well mixed, fold in the walnuts.

5. Spoon the batter over the pineapple in the skillet and bake in the preheated oven for 50 minutes, or until golden brown and a knife inserted into the cake comes out clean. Cool the cake on a rack for 15 minutes before inverting onto a serving plate. (Some of the pineapple may stick to the skillet. If so, simply remove it with a spatula and place it back on top of the cake.)

Bottom left: Lemon Meringue Pie, page 138.

Bottom right: Fresh Pineapple Upside-down Cake.

Makes 16 servings

Each serving contains approximately:

Calories: 217   **Cholesterol: None**

Fat: 7 g   **Sodium: 229 mg**

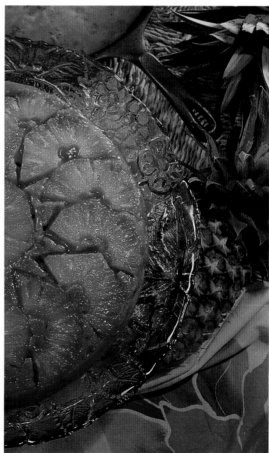

"Prudent" Pumpkin Pie

whole wheat pie crust:

1 cup whole wheat flour

1 cup unbleached all-purpose flour

$\frac{1}{2}$ teaspoon salt

$\frac{1}{3}$ cup plus 1 tablespoon canola or corn oil

$\frac{1}{3}$ cup plus 1 tablespoon low-fat liquid nondairy creamer

pie filling:

1 16-ounce can pumpkin

$\frac{2}{3}$ cup sugar

1 cup low-fat liquid nondairy creamer

1$\frac{1}{2}$ teaspoons ground cinnamon

$\frac{1}{2}$ teaspoon salt

$\frac{3}{4}$ cup water

3 tablespoons cornstarch

$\frac{1}{4}$ cup raw cashews or almonds

A few years ago I judged a nondairy recipe contest sponsored by a nondairy creamer company. This recipe was the grand prize winner.

1. Preheat the oven to 425°F. To make the crust, combine all the dry ingredients and mix well. Combine the oil and nondairy creamer and mix well.

2. Pour the liquid into the dry ingredients and mix with a fork until it forms a ball. Place the ball between two pieces of wax paper, flattening it slightly with your hands. With a rolling pin, roll into a circle $\frac{1}{8}$ inch thick and 14 inches in diameter.

3. Remove one layer of paper and place the crust in a 10-inch pie pan. Peel away the remaining paper and trim any excess dough, leaving about $\frac{1}{2}$ inch to fold and crimp around the edge of the pie.

4. To make the filling, in a large bowl whisk the pumpkin, sugar, nondairy creamer, cinnamon, and salt.

5. In a blender container, combine the water, cornstarch, and cashews or almonds. Start the blender on low and increase to high speed. Blend until very smooth (3 to 5 minutes).

6. Pour the nut mixture into the pumpkin mixture and mix again with a wire whisk. Pour the mixture into the pie crust and bake in the preheated oven for 15 minutes. Reduce the temperature to 350°F. and bake another 40 to 45 minutes, or until the filling is set and the crust is golden brown. Cool on a rack until room temperature before slicing. Store, covered, in the refrigerator.

Makes one 10-inch pie; 12 servings

Each serving contains approximately:

Calories: 230   **Cholesterol: None**

Fat: 10 g   **Sodium: 209 mg**

Apple Tarte Tatin

crust:

½ cup whole wheat flour

½ cup unbleached all-purpose
flour

1 tablespoon confectioners'
sugar

¼ teaspoon salt

2½ tablespoons cold water

6 tablespoons corn oil margarine

filling:

1¾ pounds Golden Delicious
apples (about 5 medium)

¼ cup corn oil margarine

½ cup packed dark brown
sugar

Tarte Tatin is named for two impoverished gentlewomen from the commune of Orléans in France who were forced to earn their living by baking their father's favorite upside-down pie with a caramel topping. Their exact recipe has disappeared, but the secret lies in cooking sugar in the apple juice so it caramelizes and infuses the flavor deep inside the apples. This is my lower-fat, cholesterol-free version of an old favorite.

1. To make the crust, combine all the ingredients in a food processor fitted with the dough blade until completely mixed and easily formed into a ball. Place the dough in the refrigerator, covered, to chill.

2. For the filling, peel the apples, then halve lengthwise. Carefully remove the center core with a melon baller. (Using an apple corer removes too much of the apple.)

3. In a heavy ovenproof skillet approximately 6 inches in diameter and 2½ inches deep, melt the margarine over medium heat. Add the brown sugar and slowly bring to a boil. Reduce the heat and allow to simmer slowly for 5 minutes. Remove from the heat and cool until the pan and contents are safe to handle.

4. Arrange the apple halves, upright, in a tight circle around the outside edge of the pan, "nesting" each half into the next. Fill in the center with the remaining apple halves.

5. Cook over medium heat until the sugar mixture begins to bubble up between the apples. Watch carefully to prevent the mixture from boiling over, reducing the heat if necessary. The mixture should bubble for about 20 minutes, or just until the apples can be easily pierced with a fork. Do not overcook or the apples will be mushy. Remove from the heat and allow them to cool to room temperature (or refrigerate to hasten this step).

(continued on next page)

6. Preheat the oven to 375°F. Remove the dough from the refrigerator and roll into a circle slightly larger than the top of the pan. Place the dough over the cooled apples and carefully tuck the dough in around the appples. Trim off any excess dough that sticks above the top of the pan.

7. Punch holes in the top with the tines of a fork and bake in the preheated oven for 25 to 30 minutes, or until the crust is golden brown. Remove from the oven and allow to cool slightly on a rack, at least 30 minutes.

8. To serve, turn the pan upside down onto a serving plate. (If any apples stick to the bottom of the pan, remove them and replace them on the tarte.)

Makes 6 servings

Each serving contains approximately:

Calories: 326   **Cholesterol: None**

Fat: 16 g   **Sodium: 288 mg**

"Prudent" Pumpkin Pie,
page 142.

Baked Apple Cups, page 130.

index